WAR
IN THE AIR

WAR
IN THE AIR

September 1939 — May 1941

By

DAVID GARNETT

Doubleday, Doran & Company, Inc.

GARDEN CITY *1941* NEW YORK

PRINTED AT THE *Country Life Press*, GARDEN CITY, N. Y., U. S. A.

To My Mother
CONSTANCE GARNETT

Preface

Wᴀʀ ɪꜱ ᴀ ᴅɪꜱᴀꜱᴛʀᴏᴜꜱ ɪɴᴇxᴏʀᴀʙʟᴇ ʙᴜꜱɪɴᴇꜱꜱ, *and whatever impedes a nation from developing its war effort has to be bitterly paid for in human suffering. In organizing the state for war, compulsion alone is of small value. Compulsion must rest upon the will of the people, and sacrifices may be demanded only in the degree in which a majority of the people believe them to be unavoidable."*

With those words Mr. H. A. Jones closes a chapter of the Official History of the Royal Air Force in the last war.[1] And those words explain the object of this book.

The chief obstacle to our war effort in the air has sprung from a lack of understanding of the real position by the public. At the outset of the present war, complacent ignorance of Germany's strength in the air and wishful thinking on the part of the great majority impeded the swift mobilization of our industrial power and thus assisted to bring about the German victories in the west. Ignorance today leads to a shallow optimism that shirks the need for

[1]*The War in the Air*, by H. A. Jones, Vol. VI, p. 100.

supreme sacrifices and supreme efforts, an optimism that is always likely to be followed by an even more shallow cynicism. At the same time during a war the frame of mind of Mr. Flosky in Nightmare Abbey *is one which is particularly dangerous:*

"Because all this was not done, Mr. Flosky deduced that nothing was done; and from this deduction, according to his system of logic, he drew a conclusion that worse than nothing was done."

If I have routed some of the Floskies and have made the more optimistic majority realize that victory in the air for the democracies depends not only on pilots and air marshals but on their own efforts—that it lies in the power of every citizen to help bring about a victorious conclusion to the war in the air, I shall have achieved my object.

DAVID GARNETT.

Contents

x   *Contents*

Illustrations

CHAPTER I

The Conquest of Poland

OBLIVIOUS or indifferent to the British guarantee of Polish independence, Hitler, in the summer of 1939, completed his preparations for the seizure of Danzig and the invasion of Poland. To understand the progress of the war which resulted from the German attack it is essential to remember that war with Britain and France had not been planned to take place at that time by the Nazis. Their destruction was to have come later, and their entry into the war was regarded with angry incredulity, even after it occurred, by the German leaders.

It is always hard for men to judge the ebb and flow of public opinion in a foreign country, and Germans living in a world ruled by the simple logic of force found such an estimation impossible. Yet the German invasion of Poland made war politically necessary for Britain and

France. They had to make war then if they were ever to resist the Nazi domination of Europe and the extinction of freedom in that continent. Even had there been no British guarantee of Polish independence, it is probable that public opinion would have made war inevitable then and that any Prime Minister who had acquiesced in the Nazi conquest of Poland would have been driven out of office. The long series of aggressions by the Axis powers had slowly bound the great majority of Englishmen together in a common exasperation.

Manchuria, Abyssinia, Austria, Czechoslovakia, the war in Spain, the annexation of Albania . . . Slowly the common men of the democracies had awakened to the plans for the destruction of liberty throughout the world and they were ready to resist the next piece of aggression.

But from a military point of view the war was premature. Germany did not believe that they would fight. They were not ready to fight, nor was Germany yet ready to defeat them. This unpreparedness made the war which followed partial and incomplete for many months. While it was pursued vigorously in one field, in others hostilities were not even embarked upon, because neither side was ready for them. On the Allied side unpreparedness was particularly marked in the air. It was therefore in the absence of serious air operations that unreality showed itself most strikingly.

With no realization of this unpreparedness, it was natural that to outside observers the whole war seemed suspiciously sham, and in the United States of America it was regarded as a "phony" war, and the explanation of what was so obviously "phony" was sought in political rather than in military causes. It was thus generally believed that the Germans were anxious to leave the door open to a patched-up peace and that France and Britain were likely to accept it.

Since the war opened with the German conquest of Poland, it will be best to give a brief account of the nature of that achievement before describing the "phony" war in the West.

Poland, except in the extreme south and southeast, is a large, flat country with enormous fields of corn, sugar beet, and rye, interspersed with great forests and marshes. Compared with Western Europe, there are few roads and railways, and the distances between towns are far greater. Attack upon communications is particularly effective in such a country where distances are great and communications are few. The German attack was therefore opened by the destruction of Polish communications.

The first phase of the air war was to smash up all Polish aerodromes, landing grounds, aircraft factories, and aircraft depots by simultaneous and overwhelming air attacks upon them. Secondly, the Luftwaffe was to destroy all telephone and telegraph communications by low-level bombing along the roads and railways beside which the overhead wires ran. Thirdly, at the same time as it was engaged in wrecking telephone communications the Luftwaffe was to attack the railways and to bomb and machine-gun trains and transport moving on the roads.

These plans were carried out with great rapidity and success. Only in one respect did German air attack fail. The attack on aerodromes had been planned to wipe out the Polish air force. The day before the German attack practically all serviceable Polish aircraft had been moved to secretly prepared flying fields for use in war.

The Polish air force consisted of less than five hundred aircraft, almost all of which were obsolete types. Polish Army Cooperation aircraft had a top speed of about 95 m.p.h. What possible chance had they of defending themselves effectively against German fighters which were about three and a half times as fast?

After a few days the Polish air force was almost paralyzed. Only by continually changing their stations was it possible to preserve any of their aircraft from destruction. By the fifth day of the war the Polish aircraft industry was completely out of action. By the sixth day the Polish fighter brigade was reduced from fifty-three to twenty-four aircraft.

It soon became very difficult for the Polish forces to

communicate with each other except by wireless, and after the second week it became almost impossible for anyone on the Polish side to obtain an accurate picture of what was going on in distant parts of the country.

What Polish aircraft still remained were more and more employed as the campaign went on in gathering information about the German advance—that is to say, simply in scouting.

The second duty of the Luftwaffe was army cooperation, chiefly in the form of dive-bombing attacks upon the Polish army where it had occupied strong positions and in reconnaissance. No movements of Polish troops outside the forest regions—at all events, during daylight—could be made without being observed.

The first wave of the invading German land forces consisted of tens of thousands of motorcyclists and of many thousands of automobiles, armoured cars, lorries, and tanks. The movements of all of these were directed from the air by wireless. In most cases it was a simple matter for the invaders to break through the Polish forces where they were weak, to by-pass them where they were strong, to surround them piecemeal, and to wipe them out.

The Duke of Wellington is said to have remarked that the secret of warfare is to know what your enemy is doing on the other side of the hill. The new German technique was the logical result of always knowing just that. The German generals possessed an immense superiority in the air which informed them of every movement of the enemy and the precise positions he held and they had at their disposal mechanized ground forces at least thirty miles an hour faster, on the average, than the Polish forces. It was therefore easy to split up the Poles, to penetrate far to the rear of their forces, and to divide them into units out of touch with each other and with the Higher Command. It must be remembered that the chief advantage of greater speed than your adversary in warfare is that it enables you to avoid any engagement in which you do not hold a decisive advantage. The invading Germans therefore held the initiative throughout.

It needs little imagination to realize the situation of the Poles. After a few days the telephone and telegraph wires along the main roads were everywhere interrupted by low-level bombing, and when repairs were executed the watching German aircraft returned to machine-gun working parties and bomb again.

Soon the Polish forces defending the front were running short of supplies which had been held up or destroyed by bombing on the way from the base. In air warfare base and lines of communication are more vulnerable to attack than the front, which can be isolated until it collapses. The distinction of "front" and "base" loses its meaning.

The Polish soldiers looked up, and there were the German aircraft always watching their movements and reporting their positions by wireless. Wherever the Poles held strong positions waves of German dive bombers concentrated on them and smashed them up. Paralyzed and hopelessly outclassed, masses of men and horses struggled back in a vain endeavour to form new lines of defence along the rivers. When they were split up and hemmed in by swiftly moving armoured cars and motorcycle machine-gun units they died fighting. Groups of lancers and hussars, finding themselves trapped, spurred their weary horses into a charge and, with the sun flashing on their spear points or their sabres and the dust rising, went down in heaps. And after each battue the steel hatches would be pushed open, and the young German mechanics would wipe their faces with their sweat rags and curse the red-hot barrels of their machine guns.

That was the second phase, and while it was going on—for even mechanized butchery takes time—the third phase of the work of the Luftwaffe had begun. This was the bombing of large centres of resistance, such as Warsaw.

Though greatly hampered by the difficulty of obtaining accurate information about what was going on in the greater part of western Poland, these activities of the German air force were noted, and the general methods and plan of attack were deduced in a report by the British Air Attaché in Poland. This firsthand, clear account of the German blitzkrieg methods was under consideration by the British War Office and the Air Ministry in October 1939.

The Germans were able to repeat these methods with equal success in their conquest of Holland, Belgium, and France the following summer and apparently took their adversaries in the West as much by surprise as they had the Poles.

Before a final stand against the mechanized German army could be made by the Polish forces they were taken in the rear by the Russian advance in eastern Poland. For a time Polish guerrilla bands, operating at one moment against the Germans and at the next against the Russians, continued the struggle. But the war was over, and in five weeks Poland had ceased to exist as an independent nation.

When it became obvious that further resistance was impossible the remnants of the very gallant Polish air force escaped, with every aircraft still fit for service, across the southeast frontier to Rumania. Among the large numbers of Polish soldiers and officers who likewise escaped on foot or in automobiles into Rumania there were many of the Polish air force, including mechanics and ground staff as well as pilots.

The Polish aircraft which landed in Rumania were

taken possession of by the Rumanian authorities who finally confiscated them after a considerable interval, by which time the majority, standing in the open during the winter months, had become unserviceable. The pilots and mechanics, discarding their uniforms before crossing the frontier, succeeded in escaping internment, for the Rumanian government was then timidly on the side of the Allies. After making their way through Turkey these Poles reached Syria and Egypt, and after some of them had served in France they eventually formed the nucleus of the Polish squadrons attached to the Royal Air Force and stationed in Great Britain.

A Polish estimate of the numbers of German aircraft employed during the invasion exceeds three thousand. This is possibly an overestimate. It is, however, certain, I think, that the figure of one thousand aircraft, which was believed to be roughly correct in England at the time was a considerable underestimate.

The Poles claim to have brought down 625 German aircraft during the campaign. They also claim to have brought down 127 German aircraft over Warsaw alone. These claims are made in good faith and believed by those who have arrived at the figures. Nevertheless, they may be very wide of the truth. Probably the commonest reason for believing that an aircraft has been shot down, when, in fact, it has not, is that when under accurate anti-aircraft fire the pilot takes violent avoiding action.

That is to say, the aircraft sideslips, twists, and turns as rapidly as possible, and these movements are interpreted by those on the ground as falling out of control. Such an aircraft is seen to disappear erratically behind a hill or behind trees, and those who have been firing at it are convinced that they have brought it down. They have been shooting at it, perhaps at close range, are certain they have not missed, and are convinced that they have seen it fall.

One thing which has been abundantly proved in the present war is the toughness of modern aircraft and their capacity to fly after being riddled with bullets. Unless the pilot is killed and there is no second pilot to take over, or unless all the engines are put out of action, or unless the aircraft is set on fire so badly that it cannot be extinguished by the crew, unless the cables of elevators, ailerons, or rudders are shot through, or unless a large piece of the wing, elevator, or rudder is blown off an aircraft can usually get back to its base. Again and again British bombers have returned across the North Sea on one engine, with pieces of the fuselage blown off, even with pieces of the wing gone.

Another frequent source of error is that a dozen or more reports of having shot down the same aircraft may be made independently by different parties of soldiers who were all firing at it from widely distant points when it was seen to crash. Each is certain of his claim, and not all of them may agree as to where the incident took place. If the reports come from places a dozen miles apart, which have since been occupied by the enemy's advance, it is quite impossible to be certain whether one enemy aircraft has been destroyed or a whole squadron.

Independent estimates of the German losses during their invasion of Poland were one hundred aircraft. One thing, however, must be said for the Polish claim—the quality that Polish fighter pilots have shown since in air fighting in Great Britain. They have proved themselves to be amazing fellows and have achieved a great reputation in the Royal Air Force, which, by the way, has taken the Poles to its heart. During five consecutive days in September 1940 the first Polish squadron to be formed in Britain brought down sixty-seven enemy aircraft.

Polish pilots have a reputation for holding their fire until they are almost on top of the enemy and can see the whites of his eyes. Then they shoot him to small pieces. Whatever their technique, the Poles have proved outstandingly successful, though, of course, the aircraft they fly now are very different from the ones in which they faced the Germans in September 1939.

The presence of the Polish pilots has been an education to our naturally quiet and reserved boys. A friend of mine has told me how when a Polish pilot was being transferred to another station and came to say good-bye

one after another the British pilots held out their fore-
heads for him to kiss, without a trace of self-conscious-
ness, knowing that it was a Polish custom at farewells
and anxious to make him feel less of an exile.

CHAPTER II

The "Phony" War

GREAT BRITAIN and France were at war with Germany within a few hours of the invasion of Poland. On land the results of the declaration of war were limited to the manning of the Maginot Line by the French army, together with some successful nibbling advances beyond it in the region of the Saar, which were undertaken to interfere with German coal supplies from this district.

The dispatch of a British expeditionary force, including a mechanized division and large quantities of motor transport, was successfully carried out without interference.

At sea the war resulted immediately in a blockade of the German North Sea ports and coast and the rounding up and seizure of German shipping all over the world. On the German side attacks were launched on all British and Allied shipping and on neutral shipping proceeding to British ports. The sinking of the liner, *Athenia*, without warning, by a German submarine commander was a revival of ruthless submarine warfare. In general, however, the German submarines gave warning, with time for the crews to take to the boats, before sinking merchant and fishing vessels. Frequently they took members of the vessels' crews aboard if their safety could not be otherwise ensured.

Early in this campaign vessels belonging to countries politically favouring Germany were also sunk by the U-boats if proceeding to British ports. Thus Japanese, Italian, and Spanish ships were all attacked. We shall return to the subject of German submarine attacks when we consider the work of the Coastal Command of the Royal Air Force.

It was, however, in the air that the greatest activity was anticipated. Within a few hours of the declaration of war it was expected that London and Paris would have been bombed and that large parts of them would be lying in ruins. Less-informed opinion believed that British and French help on a substantial scale would immediately be dispatched across Germany to our hard-pressed allies in Poland. Nothing of the sort occurred, and the only spectacular air operation for some time was a raid on the German fleet by British Wellington and Blenheim bombers.

In the months which followed, with no German attacks on French or British cities, air warfare assumed a peculiar lopsided aspect. The war at sea was vigorously pursued, and on both sides aircraft took an increasingly large share in it.

German aircraft bombed and machine-gunned every vessel they could find, even attacking lightships. Meanwhile British aircraft swept the seas for German submarines and attacked German surface vessels, notably in Heligoland Bight, round the Frisian Islands and in the Jade, Ems, and Elbe estuaries. Whenever British and German aircraft met in the air they attacked each other, and several German aircraft which attacked the British fleet in the Firth of Forth were shot down by British fighters, a Glasgow auxiliary squadron of the R.A.F. being notably successful.

On both sides, wherever enemy aircraft appeared, they were vigorously attacked by fighters and by anti-aircraft fire from the ground. But whereas aircraft so attacked defended themselves from attack by enemy fighters and from anti-aircraft fire from ships, they made no attempt to reply to land batteries. Nor did they ever deliberately attack any objective upon land.

The columns of French and British lorries proceeding along the roads of France and the German columns marching on the other side of the Rhine frequently offered ideal targets to hostile bomber aircraft. But neither French nor British nor German aircraft, even though making long reconnaissance flights of hundreds of miles over enemy territory, ever attacked any objectives at all.

On one occasion there was an exception to this odd immunity enjoyed by all who stood on terra firma. A British Bomber, making its run to bomb a German naval vessel lying just off the coast, came under violent and accurate anti-aircraft fire from a shore battery. One of the anti-aircraft shells exploded immediately in front of the aircraft, and the pilot swerved violently at the moment that the bomb aimer released the bomb. The effect was to throw the bomb out of the path calculated for it, and, to the surprise of those on the aircraft, it was seen to fall inshore, knocking out the anti-aircraft gun and killing its crew.

This incident was kept a close secret by the Air Ministry. For both the Allied and the German High Command considered that this "phony" war was to their advantage and were most anxious not to start warfare in real earnest.

The probable reasons for this belief on each side must be considered in some detail, for they governed the whole period up to the German invasion of Norway and the opening of total warfare in the following summer.

On the German side the arguments were probably as

follows: Although Germany possessed great numerical superiority in aircraft over the Allies, the geographical position favoured Britain in particular. So long as the R.A.F. Advanced Air Striking Force was based in northern and northeastern France it was within some 250 miles of the centre of the Ruhr district of the lower Rhineland, which is the centre of German steel, armament, shipbuilding, and synthetic-oil production. Germany might strike back at France on equal terms, but it was twice the distance from the German North Sea coast to the centres of the British armament industry—to Bristol, Coventry, and Sheffield.

It would seem, therefore, fairly obvious that it would take twice the number of German bombers to drop an equal weight of bombs on Britain as the bombers of the A.A.S.F. could drop on the Ruhr.

As a matter of fact, our advantage was greater than is revealed in that elementary calculation. Not only would every ton of bombs dropped by the A.A.S.F. cost less in petrol and in engine overhauls than the ton dropped in Britain, but the British bomber, being able to refuel after a shorter distance, could carry less petrol and more bombs—that is to say, a higher pay load of bombs than the German bomber. The cost in petrol per ton of bombs is therefore not proportional to the distance of the target from the base.

From the above we arrive at an elementary consideration which we shall have to bear in mind in discussing bombing operations. This is the cost in fuel per ton.

It is a point of particular importance to Germany owing to her limited supplies of petrol. Britain, on the other hand, so long as she can keep command of the seas and build tankers as fast as Germany can sink them, can draw on world supplies of oil.

There are two other points arising from geographical position, both of which favoured Britain. One is that bombing operations, until complete superiority over the enemy's fighters and ground defences is achieved, would probably be limited to the hours of darkness.

A German bomber attacking an objective four hundred miles from its base would take at least four and a half hours to return to its base, and it would be five hours before it could start on a second trip and seven hours before it could be again over the target.

It would therefore be unsafe for such German bombers to attempt two trips except when there were eight hours of darkness or more. The A.A.S.F. bomber in northern France could frequently do three trips when the German bomber was limited to one. For it could always employ the odd hours of darkness with a short trip to some target just over the frontier.

The desire to exploit such advantages was great among many senior officers of the Royal Air Force who were animated by a healthy offensive spirit. The R.A.F.

officers in France in particular, from the Air Marshal in command downward, chafed at being kept in idleness.

All these geographical advantages, we shall see, accrued to Germany when the positions were reversed, and the Advanced Air Striking bases of the Luftwaffe were strung along the Channel coast from Belgium to Brittany.

One geographical advantage, however, remained to Britain permanently. This was meteorological. The prevailing winds of Western Europe come in from the Atlantic. The Royal Air Force was, therefore, almost always in a better position to know weather conditions than the Luftwaffe, which was forced to send out aircraft on weather reconnaissance.

The geographical advantages which bases in northern France gave Britain were enough in themselves to make the German air staff favour a waiting policy, for the German High Command had hopes of turning the Maginot Line in due course and of occupying northern France and the Low Countries. It was therefore better for them to postpone bombing on land until they could initiate it with the geographical advantages in their favour.

The Germans may, moreover, have argued that Britain was most vulnerable at sea and that Germany presented no target comparable to the British, Allied, and neutral vessels which Germany was attacking round the British coasts and particularly in the North Sea. Germany could spend a winter of almost complete immunity while preparing her attack on the West.

Finally, if these advantages were not decisive, there was another reason of the greatest weight for postponing an air offensive on land. The German knockout blow on the Western front was not ready. They wished to have their air force, which would play the leading role in this offensive as it had in Poland, at its highest strength when the blow was delivered and they wished it to come as a surprise. Its losses were bound to be very heavy.

On the British and French side the arguments for delay seem at first sight weaker from the point of view of logical strategy. But they were no less cogent than the German.

The defensive policy adopted by the Allied War Council was imposed upon them, owing to their own unpreparedness and weakness. This may, in certain respects, be regarded as a grievous fault but, in the main, it was the inevitable result of their being peaceful democracies. Thoroughly to prepare and equip a nation for war as Germany had been equipped is impossible in time of peace except under a dictatorship. Even with a united people behind him and with the fate of all the democratic countries staring the American people in the face, it has proved necessary for Mr. Roosevelt to assume semidictatorial powers in order that the United States should rearm. And even so, we do not know whether it will be possible for the United States to arm in time. But Britain and France were bent, not on rearmament, but on disarmament at the time when Hitler and Goering began to build up German armaments. The policy of appeasement commanded the assent of the majority of men of all parties. The politicians who openly favoured rearmament were rare and they were not in power.

Thus France and Britain, when they declared war, were short of all war equipment. While they were training their armies they had, at all costs, to put off an offensive. It must be realized that it was not only in aircraft that the Germans had superiority. In tanks, guns, machine guns, and every kind of military vehicle they were better equipped than the Allies. Their armament factories were all in full production. The Allied factories had to be adapted or new ones built. Many of them would not come into production for eighteen months.

The British were indeed so short of rifles and small-arm ammunition that carbines and ammunition dating from the Boer War were served out to the crews of motorboats patrolling the Thames estuary.

In 1919 the victorious Allies had millions of rifles of

their own patterns and millions of German rifles surrendered under the peace treaty in their hands; they had machine guns in tens of thousands. These would have made all the difference to the rapid training of their armies, but in the moment of victory they never thought of danger ever threatening them again, and the rifles and machine guns which would have held back the Germans were scattered over China and Abyssinia. The Boer War carbines had been retained simply because they were worth nothing. There was no people so backward as to be ready to buy such antiquities. Thus when the Germans broke through to the Channel ports the British people who rose to fight in the last ditch against the invaders would have had to fight with twelve-bore shotguns.

This inferiority in armament was not, of course, realized by the peoples of the democracies. For example, the combined strengths of the Royal Air Force and of the Armée de l'Air in up-to-date aircraft were greatly below those of the Luftwaffe. And the Allied ground defences against aircraft were also greatly inferior in numbers to the German. Yet these facts were not known, and it was generally accepted by the public that the British and French air forces combined were at least equal to the German. It was believed that German output could be easily equalled and overtaken by purchases from the United States, which was commonly believed to have the largest aircraft industry of any country in the world. This was very far from being the case.

The Allied Supreme War Council, therefore, was anxious to postpone every form of offensive for as long as possible. Nobody knew what would happen when air war began in real earnest. The danger of a collapse of public morale when the facts as to German superiority came out were very real. Everything pointed to the desirability of postponing the evil day.

Such were the opinions of Gamelin and of most of the other French generals, and, if only for that reason, arguments on the other side stood no chance of prevailing.

Yet it is worth while to glance at them. Now that we are made wise by the event they appear more impressive than when deference to the superior wisdom of French military leadership and knowledge was a legacy from the last war and when all of us amateurs had been influenced by Captain Liddell Hart's brilliant expositions of the advantages which accrue to the defensive.

The arguments for an air offensive against Germany during the months of waiting are for the most part implicit in those which influenced the German High Command to defer their offensive against us. That is to say, the Germans were not ready; our strategic offensive would delay their preparations, and the geographical advantages were on our side.

This last argument would have only been ruefully ad-mitted by a Frenchman, since although the Germans could not bomb Birmingham as readily as we could bomb Essen they could revenge themselves with a double dose on Lille. And the Allied commander-in-chief was a Frenchman.

There is one argument which military theorists seem rather to have overlooked when considering the ad-vantages of the defensive. That is the moral qualities involved. It is exceedingly difficult for man to await his enemy's moves with the perfect confidence of the cat waiting for the mouse. There is too much of the mouse in his make-up. When we have only the mouse's (or perhaps it would be fairer to say the rat's) armament it is impossible to maintain feline morale through months of waiting. Indeed, it is difficult to have the cat's arro-gant assurance even when we enjoy her superior strength. And in that case the defensive becomes unnec-essary. On the other hand, the mere assumption of the offensive gives man courage, and in the winter months of 1939 and 1940 a spirit of courageous impudence and activity, rather than waiting about to get cold feet, was what was needed. The French army in particular had too much leisure in which to reflect on the inconven-iences of war and to swallow the bait of German propa-ganda.

It is possible that, had an air offensive against Germany been carried out at this period, it would have quickened a warlike and offensive spirit in the French army and that German bombing of French cities would have aroused a fighting spirit in the French. It would certainly have made Nazi propaganda which kept repeating that Germany wanted nothing from France more difficult.

Anything of the sort was vetoed by Gamelin, and, though we now see the evils of his policy, I cannot help believing that, owing to our unpreparedness, he was right, and that waiting was the only policy to pursue.

From the point of view of mobilizing Britain's war effort, it was, however, doubly unfortunate that the public was led to believe that a vast expansion of the Royal Air Force was taking place when the Luftwaffe was really growing in size at a much greater rate than the British and French air forces put together. During the months of waiting the Germans were becoming relatively far stronger in aircraft than they were when war was declared. Since an air offensive was vetoed by the French, owing to Allied weakness, that weakness should discreetly have been made known. To make it known was the only method of remedying it by a reorganization of the aircraft industry. Even Parliament was kept in ignorance of the truth.

This was a dangerous mistake.

It is folly to believe that wars can be won without a

supreme effort. Every man and woman in Britain and the British Dominions will have to pay for victory, not only passively by the sacrifice of money and of luxuries but by long hours of toil. Free men and women will do this. When they realize that it is not only their happiness which is at stake but the freedom and even the existence of their children they will work harder, suffer more, and fight longer than the most disciplined robots of the Fascist states. Anything which helps the citizens of our democracy to believe that victory is easy is treason, for all men are ready to relax, to resume their indulgences, to believe that victory will come magically, owing to victories in the past or even (so blind is faith) owing to the wisdom and foresight of their rulers.

Thus, owing to timidity which prevented them from taking their peoples into their confidence, the governments of the democracies wasted much of the first eight months of the war. The Germans did not.

CHAPTER III

The R. A. F. before the War

Unlike the air force of the United States, the Royal
Air Force is an arm totally distinct from the army and
the navy and independent of either. The simplest and
most important way of expressing this independence is
by saying that British airmen are no more soldiers than
are the bluejackets of the navy. In dress, discipline, attitude of mind, as well as in their work, British airmen
are unlike the men who belong to the older services.
The air, like the sea, attracts or produces its own type
of man. Later I shall have the opportunity of letting
some of these men speak for themselves, and the reader
will learn some of the factors which make it what it is.
Here I only wish to underline that the Royal Air Force
is an independent body made up of and commanded by
men who are not soldiers and not sailors but airmen.

This independence was achieved with difficulty and both in peace and war has been assailed in Parliament and in the press. The campaign against an independent air force has been waged chiefly by retired admirals and generals who wished Britain to revert to the United States' model of two air forces, each forming a branch of the arm it serves. That was the position in the British service in the early years of the war of 1914–18. The Royal Flying Corps and the Royal Naval Air Service were distinct forces—so distinct that they competed against each other in ordering their equipment from the aircraft industry. They competed in other ways also, and, thanks to the vision and imagination of that great statesman and soldier, General Smuts, during the last year of the war the two air branches were successfully amalgamated. Thus the Royal Air Force was created and welded together during the heat of the battle by the needs of war. The creation of an independent air force was indeed one of the most important military results of the last war. The agitation against an independent air force was so great, however, that in 1937 the Fleet Air Arm of the Royal Navy was created and put under the admiralty. This consists of aircraft flown from aircraft carriers and used in naval reconnaissance and fleet operations. Some shore-based squadrons of the Fleet Air Arm were for a time put under the direction of the Coastal Command of the Royal Air

Force in order to secure unity of command shortly after war broke out.

The war of 1914–18 ended with the destruction or surrender of the entire German air force. During the years 1914–18 it had at times been the superior of the British and French air forces, particularly as regards the performance of its fighters, and though by the autumn of 1918 it had been outbuilt, outclassed, and outnumbered by the combined air forces of Britain, France, and the United States it had yet inflicted greater losses than it had itself suffered. This was partly the result of the policy pursued by the officers commanding the Royal Air Force acting under the orders of the British commander in chief, Sir Douglas Haig.

When the war was over a plan drawn up by the air staff under Sir Frederick Sykes of an air force of 154 squadrons was set aside, and a program of twenty-four and a half squadrons for the entire British Empire was adopted.

This is not the place to tell the history of the Royal Air Force in the years of peace. Yet it is not enough to say that when Lord Trenchard became Chief of Air Staff in 1919 Britain was the first air power in the world and that when he left in 1930 she had sunk to fifth, for this decrease must not be regarded as Trenchard's doing. The plain fact is that British politicians had been brought up with an understanding of the importance of sea power. There was no such understanding of the importance of air power, and public opinion in Great Britain would not have consented to the expenditure necessary for maintaining supremacy in the air as well as at sea. The public mind was indeed greatly agitated by the number of accidents which occurred in training in the Royal Air Force, though these were never comparable to those in Germany during the creation of the Luftwaffe.

Typical of the British politicians' attitude during these years to the subject of air power was that of Sir Samuel Hoare. When Secretary of State for Air he justified the curtailment of the air estimates as showing the desire of the British government to give a lead in disarmament. Yet within a year of his being out of office he was calling for air parity for Britain with any other great power.

It may be argued that the decline in the size of the Royal Air Force and its relative weakness were unimportant during the existence of the German Republic, even though at that time the Soviet Union was equipping itself with an air force of tremendous size and the Japanese air force was being rapidly expanded.

For it may be argued that in these years the only likelihood of the British Empire being involved in war was in conjunction with a number of allies when called upon to defend a fellow member of the League of Nations from aggression.

Against this it may be stated that the lack of an adequate British air force was one of the factors which led to the collapse of the system of collective security which seemed so admirable until it was tested by events. The system revealed its hollowness when Japan invaded Manchuria and set up the puppet government of Manchukuo. The real test came when Italy, which had three years before sponsored Abyssinia as a member of the League of Nations, declared war upon that country without the shadow of an excuse. Sanctions were imposed, for the British government, forced by public opinion, took a stronger line against Italy than it had against Japan. And Sir Samuel Hoare, who, together with M. Laval, planned appeasement of the Fascist states at the expense of Abyssinia, had to retire into private life for a period, and Mr. Eden became Foreign Secretary.

As a result Italy came near to declaring war against Britain. Had oil been declared a contraband, Italy could not have carried on the Abyssinian war and would have declared war on Britain. The British navy was not at that time adequately equipped against air attack, and the Royal Air Force was too small for Britain to be able to face a war. Whatever the immediate results in the

Mediterranean of such a war, there is not the slightest doubt that Italy would have been eventually defeated, and it is unlikely that Mussolini would have survived as Duce to declare war upon Great Britain and France in their hour of greatest need in the summer of 1940.

The scale of the cutting-down of the Royal Air Force during the years of peace may be thought to be partly due to the fact that it was the youngest and least influential of the services. But it is most unlikely that, had the system of flying branches of the army and the navy been retained, a penny more would have been spent on them or on aviation. The British military attitude to air power can be judged by that of the commander in chief in France. In September 1918 Mr. Winston Churchill wrote to Lloyd George: "If Haig had to choose fifty thousand men for the infantry or fifty thousand men for the air force he would choose fifty thousand men for the infantry."

Haig will be longest remembered for the battle of the Somme. On the first day of that battle there were sixty thousand British casualties. The battle lasted for months, so Haig naturally needed infantry. Seven years after the war Haig announced at a public dinner that airplanes and tanks were only accessory to the man and the horse and that as time went on he felt sure that they would find as much use for the horse—the well-bred horse—as they had ever done in the past.

It may be regarded as unfair to the British army to quote its commander in chief's words as an example of informed military opinion. Nevertheless, until the German break through in France in 1940 few British soldiers had any conception of the importance of air power or of the part it would play in revolutionizing warfare. Such understanding has been, if anything, rarer among naval officers. It is possible that one reason for this has been that the Royal Air Force drew to itself most officers of imagination and originality from the older services when it was first formed. The lack of "air-minded" soldiers and sailors of the older generation is the price paid by the Royal Air Force for its independence.

We have seen that while Trenchard was Chief of Air Staff the Royal Air Force declined relatively to the air forces of other powers and that this decline was inevitable. The effects of this decline might have been fatal had it not been for the far-sighted lines on which the Royal Air Force was built up by Trenchard and the brothers John and Geoffrey Salmond during their periods of administration.

First in importance was the policy pursued in recruiting the Royal Air Force. This policy is mainly responsible for its character today.

We have seen that its officers were originally drawn from soldiers and sailors who volunteered for the Royal

Flying Corps or the Royal Naval Air Service, and many
who now hold high rank entered the Royal Air Force
in this way. Similarly, its non-commissioned officers had
often held equivalent rank in the army or the navy.
But, once established, Trenchard aimed at making the
Royal Air Force a really democratic service, seeking
his material in the most mechanically gifted and air-
minded of every class, without social or money qualifi-
cations. By this policy it was made easy for boys from
the grammar and secondary schools as well as from the
famous public schools to enter the Royal Air Force,
either directly or through Cadet College Cranwell, and
to obtain commissions. But, while the officers were thus
drawn from a wider cross-section of the community
than those of either the navy or the army, a higher
standard was required among the rank and file. The
British army was traditionally officered by the upper
classes but manned by misfits who had failed in civil
life. Scarcely one in a thousand enlisted because he was
keen on the job or hoped to better himself by having
been a private soldier in the army. In contrast to this, no
man was welcome to the Royal Air Force unless he was
eager to learn a mechanical trade or to fly or to rise to
better things by means of the Royal Air Force than he
could achieve outside it. The technical side had provided thousands of young men with the best mechanical
training in the world. Thus, if compared with the older

services, the Royal Air Force is officered and manned by young men picked because of a certain thrusting ability, all of whom are anxious to do well for themselves in the world of today. No officer has accepted a commission in the Royal Air Force with weary resignation because it was expected of him by family tradition. No man has enlisted with shame because he had failed as a workman or because he was an outcast from his social group. And in most cases the Royal Air Force recruit was encouraged to think of his service, not as a career, but as a steppingstone to some later occupation for which it would fit him.

Some of the more conventional officers of the Royal Air Force were perpetually worried by the fact that airmen lack, and, indeed, have a contempt for, the mechanical discipline of a regiment of the guards. Such officers, not always the keenest pilots or the most brilliant engineers, love the ceremonial of arms drill and the precision of saluting and attribute mystical moral qualities to these military practices. It was a dark day for such disciplinarians when Trenchard, at the suggestion of a serving aircraftman, abolished the useless bayonet and the walking-out cane.

But when the real test came, when France was collapsing in May 1940, it was found that our airmen did as well as guardsmen. When our forward aerodromes had hastily to be evacuated, with German tanks within a few miles of them, strings of R.A.F. lorries were often sent off at a moment's notice, without officers and without interpreters, by some unknown route to a new destination. Thanks to the innate independence of the airmen of the R.A.F., they always got there, when the most disciplined soldiers would have been lost.

Under Trenchard's administration the system of short-service commissions was developed, by which a large reserve of qualified pilots was built up. Squadrons of the Auxiliary Air Force Reserve, comparable to units of the territorial army, were established at the universities of Oxford and Cambridge and in the vicinity of large towns, and flying clubs were subsidized. By this means the Royal Air Force would, in the event of war, be able to call upon the services of a large number of trained or partly trained pilots. The same system was adopted with regard to the non-commissioned officers who were not allowed to re-enlist or to extend their terms of service.

One other factor of immense importance in the early days of the Royal Air Force must be mentioned. It was a decision made by Winston Churchill, on the advice of T. E. Lawrence and Trenchard when creating the kingdom of Irak, by which the Royal Air Force became responsible for the preservation of order, the army being withdrawn. The system of air control in Irak was a double benefit to the British taxpayer. It was

a great economy in money, and Irak was an ideal training ground for the Royal Air Force and was its great
opportunity.

A good deal of nonsense is often talked about the
Royal Air Force bombing tribesmen. In Irak tribes
which raided their neighbours or the settled areas were
punished by bombing after twenty-four hours' warning
had been given. In practice this involved no more than
the loss of property and not loss of life. When tribesmen
on the borders of the British Empire raid for cattle or
women no law of chivalry binds us to fight them with
their own weapons.

Owing to the Royal Air Force responsibilities in Irak
and to risings on the N.W. frontier of India and dis-
turbances in Palestine, a very large number of senior
officers of the Royal Air Force had seen active service
before war broke out in 1939. They were thus able to
meet the Germans who had served with General
Franco's forces in Spain and the Italians who had defeated the Abyssinians and had also seen service in
Spain on fairly equal terms.

During what we may call "the starvation period"
Air Ministry policy with regard to scientific advances
in aviation had been uniformly good and has remained
good.

In the early days of aviation the biplane had proved
itself the most practical type of aircraft. Its advantage

is that it is an easier engineering problem to secure rigidity, strength, and lightness by bracing two thin planes together with wire than to build one plane with no external bracing. Weight for weight, a box construction is the stronger. The biplane, however, is inherently slower than the monoplane. Experimental work on the construction of thick-winged monoplanes made most progress in Germany and Holland, and the problem was first successfully solved by giving the structure a thick and tough skin which in the first place (as in the Klemm) was of plywood instead of fabric. Such a method naturally led on to all-metal construction. The advantage of the monoplane is in its very much higher speed. At the same time the slotted leading edge, which had extended the speed range of aircraft, was developed into the flapped trailing edge. This enabled high-speed monoplanes to have safe landing speeds. The reason why the world's speed record had been always held by seaplanes was that until the invention of the flap high-speed monoplanes could not safely alight on land, though they could on water.

The two Schneider·Cup contests between the British and Italian air forces in 1929 and 1931 were of the greatest importance in the development of aircraft and engine design. They are an outstanding instance of engineering research work being financed in the name of sport and patriotism. The appeal that Great Britain must keep the speed record of the air produced the funds from a patriotic and simple-minded woman who would never have subsidized scientific research. The work done in connection with the Schneider Cup came at a most important time and resulted in the Royal Air Force being equipped with the best fighters in the world in 1939. The late R. J. Mitchell designed the S6 Supermarine which, with the Rolls-Royce R engine, gave a speed of 328.6 m.p.h. in 1929 and which in 1931, with the same engine boosted up, made a speed record of 407 m.p.h. In 1934 the Air Ministry decided to abandon the biplane fighter in favour of a heavily armoured monoplane. Mitchell then designed the Spitfire which was the direct outcome of his experience with the S series of seaplanes built for the Schneider Cup.

Mr. Sydney Camm, chief designer of Hawker aircraft, designed the Hurricane at about the same time, though it was not until 1938 that the first squadron of the R.A.F. was equipped with it.

The facts regarding German rearmament in the air after Hitler came into power were not recognized and were frequently denied by Mr. Baldwin, then Prime Minister, in answer to repeated questions on the subject by Winston Churchill. Finally the British Cabinet took alarm, and the expansion of the Royal Air Force was begun, but it was begun too late and on an insufficient scale. On the other hand, the expansion was on the right lines, and very few serious mistakes were made. Perhaps the siting of some of the new aerodromes and their stereotyped layout was the worst blunder. Many proved liable to flooding; most were built where they were overlooked from a main road, and the hangars and buildings were laid out so as to be conspicuous from the air and inherently difficult to camouflage. But if the aerodromes of that period are open to criticism, the aircraft and the training of the men who were to fly them were both beyond all praise.

When in September 1938 the crisis came over Czechoslovakia the Royal Air Force was in a transitional condition, and the superiority of the German air force made war out of the question. In these circumstances Mr. Neville Chamberlain flew to Munich and after a meeting with Hitler came back announcing that he brought "peace in our time." Though that proved to be an overstatement, he did bring an absolutely necessary breathing space, and the re-equipping and rearmament of the Royal Air Force and also of the army was vigorously proceeded with.

In the expansion of the Royal Air Force which followed on the creation of the German air force three technical decisions of far-reaching importance were adopted.

A power-driven gun turret was incorporated in the design of all British long-range bombing aircraft. The disadvantage of the turret was that it interfered with streamlining and thus reduced the speed of the aircraft and subjected it to strains which might be dangerous near the stall. This was notably the case in aircraft in which turrets were added as an afterthought. But the power-driven turret, though it reduced the speed of the British bomber, enabled it to defend itself from attack on far better terms than the bomber in which the rear gunner sat in a cockpit and had to operate his gun by hand. The power-driven turret could also be armed with a number of synchronized guns. Thanks to their turrets, British bombers proved well able to defend themselves from fighter attack, whereas the German bombers such as the Heinkel 111 were extremely vulnerable to beam attack.

Almost equal in importance to the adoption of the gun turret in the British bomber was the armament of eight synchronized machine guns arranged in the leading edges of the wings in the single-seater fighters.

This was the most powerful armament of any fighter aircraft in the world and enabled the British Spitfires and Hurricanes to pour a terrific fire on their opponents. Many instances have occurred when the fire from the eight machine guns of a Spitfire has actually cut through the fuselage of a German bomber, severing the tail as though with a buzz saw.

The third wise decision was the purchase of some

hundreds of aircraft from the United States. In practice this meant the purchase for Britain of a twin-engined Lockheed monoplane slightly adapted from a type much used on American air lines. It is an airplane with a high speed, obtained by the combination of two powerful engines and tapering wings of small area. The faults of its high-wing loading for military purposes are that it has a high landing speed and poor manoeuvrability, and these faults were probably increased after it had been fitted with a power-driven turret in the afterpart of the fuselage.

It is known in this form as the "turreted Hudson," and the whole of this type was allocated to the Coastal Command of the Royal Air Force where they gave and are giving invaluable service.

No United States fighter aircraft was bought before the outbreak of war for the Royal Air Force in quantity, but the French Armée de l'Air was fortunate in obtaining some hundreds of Curtiss fighters.

Hitler came into power in 1933, but the creation of the German air force had begun at an even earlier date. It is so intimately bound up with Hermann Goering that it is perhaps useful to remind the reader of the chief facts as to his career and to give an estimate of his character. Goering was born in 1893 and brought up as a child in his grandfather's castles in Bavaria. Entering the army as a sublieutenant in 1912, he became

an observer in the German flying corps in 1914. After
the death of the great German ace, Baron Manfred von
Richthofen, he became the leader of what was known
to the Allies as "Richthofen's circus."

Mr. H. A. Jones in the official history of the Royal
Air Force in the Great War[1] tells us that under Goering's leadership the squadron suffered such severe losses
that it never recovered its glory.

"Many of the aircraft were in the air on the eighth of
August, taking part in combat after combat. . . . The
squadron was reduced in a short time from fifty airplanes to eleven. Hermann Goering rallied the remnants of the squadron and again took them into the
air, but four more airplanes were lost. The 'Richthofen
circus' which for nearly two years had been the head
and front of the German air-fighting formations in the
West had been fought almost to destruction. What remained of it was withdrawn from the battle."

Mr. Jones attributes the eclipse of the squadron to
Goering's recklessly offensive temperament which he
contrasts with that of Manfred von Richthofen, who
never hesitated to avoid or break off combat if the conditions appeared to him to be too unfavourable.

At the time of the armistice Goering refused to surrender the aircraft of his squadron and flew it back to

[1]*The War in the Air*, Vol. VI, p. 443.

Germany. After this period he is said to have become a morphine addict and a drug trafficker.

He joined the Nazi party in 1922, was wounded in the Putsch of 1923, and was elected to the Reichstag in 1928. In 1931 he formed the National German Air Association, by means of which the Nazi party obtained virtual control of German aviation. Under cover of the widespread enthusiasm for gliding and of the Gliding and Light airplane clubs he made the Hitler Youth air-minded and created a large body of trained and half-trained pilots.

When Hitler came into power in 1933 Goering became Minister for Air and immediately began to build the German Air Force with the utmost haste from these early foundations. This was, of course, a breach of the Treaty of Versailles, but few people in England cared to know the facts which were frequently denied by Mr. Baldwin, then Prime Minister. He may have been misinformed by his technical advisers, but it would be interesting to know who was to blame.

Ambassador Dodd, who was United States representative at Berlin from 1933 to 1937, wrote in his diary that Goering was fat and cruel and that he didn't like him, and this, I think, would be the estimate of all decent people who are not blinded by admiration of power and efficiency. Goering is an example of a combination which is more frequent in nature than in litera-

LAME DUCK COMES HOME

A *Lockheed Hudson* of the R.A.F. Coastal Command received direct hits from anti-aircraft guns when on reconnaissance over Norway. Shells pierced both wings and shrapnel spattered the fuselage, starboard, engine, rudders and punctured the right tire. A petrol tank was holed and many gallons of petrol were lost. In spite of all these disabilities, the machine was piloted home safely to her base on one engine but with her crew unhurt.

ture: a brave bully and a braggart. Almost immediately after the Nazis came into power the Reichstag building was burned down. It is almost universally believed by those who have studied the evidence that the fire was due to Goering's instigation and connivance. An assortment of Communists was rounded up and charged with the crime, and Goering cross-examined the accused. When one of them, the Bulgarian Dimitrov, showed no fear of him Goering lost control of himself and threatened him with what would be done to him in prison afterwards. This was in open court. Second thoughts seem to have shown the Nazis that to maltreat this prisoner during his trial would create a bad impression. Dimitrov was, in fact, acquitted and released. He shortly afterwards became head of the Comintern, or Communist International, in Moscow and is still an intimate of Stalin.

Goering has the geniality of most fat, self-indulgent Bavarians, and this and his tremendous force of character have made him the most popular man in Germany today.

As has been elsewhere indicated, the speed of German rearmament proved to be not an unmixed benefit. By starting from scratch the Germans were able to lay out their aircraft factories equipped with the latest machinery for mass production and sited with a view to their defence in war. But it left them with little time for experiment and inclined to take far-reaching decisions too quickly. Moreover, the Nazi tyranny, the persecution of liberals and Jews, had disastrous results upon German scientific work. Original research work in the German language within the Reich dropped by over a third in almost all branches of science in the years after Hitler came into power. This decline has continued ever since and has been measured objectively by the decrease in the number of pages published in reputable scientific journals. The quality of German scientific work as well as the quantity is said to have gone down. This, however, cannot be measured. During the same period there has been an abnormal increase in the volume of research work published in the United States of America. There was also an increase in that published in Britain and France.

The Nazis did all in their power to foster aeronautical engineering, and there was no decline in German research in that. But today the sciences are so closely connected that research work in mathematics and physics frequently has an immediate bearing on military problems or practical engineering. The ignorance, narrowness, and intolerance of Nazi beliefs handicapped their rearmament, and in various ways the German air force is paying the price today.

Ernst Udet was a pilot in the Richthofen squadron under Goering's leadership and was credited with sixty-

two confirmed victories in the air. After the war he became a stunt pilot with the Ufa film company and gave
aerobatic exhibitions in the U.S.A. In 1936 he was appointed by Goering director of research and development in the German air force. Udet was therefore
largely responsible for the German choice of aircraft
types. He decided that the German bomber should rely
upon speed, evasion, and fighter escort for protection
rather than upon its defensive armament. For the same
reasons he preferred medium-sized twin-engined bombers to larger types which he believed would be too vulnerable as targets. He also concluded that air battles
would take the form of stern chases and that the fighter
should be the fastest possible aircraft, with only a forward armament.

Fortunately for Britain, the first of these decisions, at
any rate, has been proved to be a serious mistake. German bombers of the type chosen have been, as we shall
see, shot down in very large numbers simply because of
the weakness of their defensive armament. At the beginning of 1939 Udet was appointed Director General of
Equipment and Supply, in which he became responsible
for production and distribution as well as for research.
He has since been promoted to the rank of a full general.
Udet has been described as an amusing, versatile, and
likeable man. He made it a point of honor to test each
new type of aircraft built for the G.A.F. personally.

This was probably the job he was best qualified to do. Udet is credited with being responsible for a number of German mistakes. The Me. 109 was originally designed for a 600-h.p. engine. It proved too slow, so a much bigger engine was installed. Weights had then to be put into the tail, the wing loading went up, and the Me. 109 became difficult to manoeuvre, particularly on right-hand turns.

Again German fighters, as well as bombers, were insufficiently armed, and no armour was provided for the protection of the pilot.

German engineers made two improvements of importance in military aircraft before the war. They perfected a self-sealing petrol tank which would not leak after it had been pierced by a bullet. They also did away with the carburetor by injecting petrol direct into the engine cylinders. The great advantage of this improvement to Germany is that it permits the use of aviation spirit of lower octane number than is required by the engines of British aircraft. It helps to economize German oil reserves.

The following remarks on the French air force may sound ungenerous to a much-loved and gallant ally. But it is only by recognizing the mistakes of the French that we can understand why they were defeated. There is no doubt that the Armée de l'Air was much below the Royal Air Force in organization and training. Its senior officers were not practical men but theorists. They were capable of brilliant projects but were not from their own experience always aware of what was possible. Thus on one occasion when both British and French reconnaissance aircraft were ordered to collect certain information French senior officers showed surprise that the British aircraft had brought it in. They had been told that the weather was too bad.

The French Air Staff had nothing comparable to the British detailed plans for a strategic offensive and seemed to British officers to know little about the employment of bombers. This was perhaps because the defensive attitude of mind ran through the French army from the commander in chief downwards. They were at all times loathe to provoke the enemy. From the first they were more alive to the need for fighters to protect their troops from bombing than were the British and before the battle began in May they made several requests to the British Air Ministry that more fighters should be sent to France.

One of the greatest weaknesses of the French was that the commanding officer seldom knew what was going on, as their system of communications had not progressed since 1918. Information gathered by their air reconnaissance did not reach headquarters until it was too late to be of use. This was, of course, not the fault of their pilots but of the organization on the ground.

Finally, though the Armée de l'Air was weak in numbers it was congested in distribution, as the French had too few aerodromes and these lacked satellite landing grounds in their vicinity. As the Germans pushed forward into France the congestion became worse and the efficiency of the Armée de l'Air became less and less. Owing to this congestion, I believe that during the battle of France more French aircraft were destroyed by the Germans on the ground than in the air.

CHAPTER IV

R. A. F. and G. A. F. Compared

THE ORGANIZATION of the Royal Air Force is simple. It is divided into commands, each of which in Britain is responsible for work of a distinct kind. Overseas Commands are responsible for all air operations within a definite area. The commands with which I shall have to deal most are Bomber, Fighter, and Coastal. There are also in Britain two Training Commands, operational and technical, and the Balloon Command. There are also the Overseas Commands: such was the British air force in France; such are the Middle Eastern and the Far Eastern Commands.

Each command consists of headquarters staff and of a certain number of groups. The group may contain a varying number of squadrons, and the squadron may contain a varying number of aircraft. In general it may be assumed that each station is commanded by a group captain.

But, while some stations are purely bomber stations or fighter stations, others are mixed and are shared by bomber and fighter squadrons.

While everyone in the Royal Air Force tends to acquire certain characteristics in common, there is a noticeable difference between the average fighter and bomber pilots. This is partly due to innate differences, men of a certain temperament being more useful in one capacity than in the other, and it is partly due to the effect of the work itself upon the men who do it.

The bomber is flown by a crew of three to five men. They depend upon each other for long hours, often under terrible weather conditions. Each one has his own specialized job and normally does not go outside it. For the crew to be a happy one each man must have complete confidence in each of his companions. If there is a weak link in the chain all suffer. Against this danger must be set the enormous advantages of the team spirit and the mutual support of each other's presence, which alone renders the long hours and the intense cold endurable.

The fighter pilot is in most cases alone in his aircraft. He has a greater strain on him because he has simultaneously to carry out the duties of pilot, navigator, wireless operator, and gunner. Loneliness, particularly at high altitudes, is itself a strain for certain types of men. For others it is a relief, but the fighter pilot can never enjoy the healing sense of peace, of having escaped for a little while from the world below, which is the gift of the air enjoyed by the solitary pilot in time of peace. At every instant he must watch for the enemy. Every moment is one of tension. He is alert, expectant, ready to meet and forestall attack.

This intense strain on the attention which must never for one second be relaxed is mitigated by the fact that usually he flies in company and, if not actually in formation, usually knows that he has companions at hand. But what makes the strain endurable is the knowledge that in less than two hours from his taking off he will be back on the ground. Under normal conditions his duty will have been done and he will be free for the rest of the day. The game of squash or tennis, the picnic on the river, the book he has been reading, or the girl he is looking forward to meeting are only divided from him by sixty or ninety minutes of time. Finally he has what to certain types is the enormous comfort of knowing that his is the entire responsibility and that he alone will pay the price of his mistakes.

Such a reflection is not actually true, since fighter pilots flying in formation are responsible for each other's safety. Yet it is psychologically true, simply because the fighter pilot is alone in his aircraft.

Bomber and Coastal Command pilots are sobered by the sense of responsibility for the safety of their crews and of their aircraft and have the patient fortitude that comes of long endurance. Fighter pilots are more highly strung, more reckless, quicker in their nervous responses and more at the mercy of their moods. They live in a world that is constantly changing colour.

As I have said already, the difference in education, intelligence, and background is less between the officers and men of the Royal Air Force than in either the navy or the army. Since the war began all officers, with few exceptions, are promoted from the ranks. The chief difference that one notices is one of temperament. Royal Air Force officers are rather gay; the airmen are serious.

It is clearly impossible for an Englishman to make a dispassionate comparison of the men of the Royal Air Force and those of the Luftwaffe. One can get some idea perhaps by contrasting the creators of each—Trenchard and Goering.

Of Lord Trenchard I may say that under no circumstances of national disaster or political expediency can he be conceived of as prosecuting a stray alien for a crime he had himself committed or of threatening him with maltreatment when he got him out of court if the evidence the man gave were not to his liking.

Of Reichsmarschall Goering I may say that under no circumstances can he be conceived of as writing the letter Trenchard wrote to T. E. Lawrence on April 10, 1928, when he was Chief of Air Staff and Lawrence was a second-class aircraftman in the Royal Air Force. It expressed Trenchard's deep regret at the Royal Air Force being involved in trying to put down raiding by Ibn Saud's partisans on the settled districts of Irak, since people who spent their lives raiding in a traditional manner could not be expected to understand our point of view and our methods of bombing from the air seemed brutal to them.

A more chivalrous and humane letter it has seldom been my privilege to read.

Goering's attitude to a very different kind of bombing is on record. Generalfeldmarschall Sperrle, who was a technical air adviser on the German staff in 1914, established his claim to greatness by the destruction of the little Basque town of Guernica during his command of the Condor Legion in the Spanish Civil War.

On his return to Germany, Sperrle was promoted to the rank of full general over the heads of others and presented by Goering with a special flying badge of gold set with diamonds.

His experiment with Guernica undoubtedly fits him for the later job of directing operations against Bristol and the west of England. Like Goering, Sperrle is bulky, with a brutal face.

I will not embarrass any of the serving senior officers

of the Royal Air Force by contrasting them with Feld-marschall Sperrle.

As for the pilots, it is impossible to speak. The quietness, gentleness and charm of all those I have met or flown with has struck me with surprise. There was no brusqueness at their work, nor rowdiness off duty. Above all, there was an absence of affectation very surprising in young men. Responsibility must have knocked it out of them.

No doubt there are some pretty tough chaps in the Royal Air Force, for toughness is needed today. And there must be some decent material in the German air force. But the training and background—what anthropologists call the *ethos* of Hitler's Germany—is so remote from British standards that quite different qualities must be brought out.

A curious feature of the German air force in the war of 1914–18 was that an aping of the British was fashionable. Directly the German pilots got to know of any custom in clothes or habits in vogue in the Royal Flying Corps they imitated it often in face of the disapproval of senior German officers.

Some such sense of the superiority of British prestige led Hitler to assume the toothbrush moustache characteristic of the British subaltern in the Great War and to dress himself in an imitation of the British or American officer's tunic—brown like khaki in colour and with breast pockets—and to gird himself with a leather Sam Browne belt.

In this imitation of the victorious enemy's uniform he no doubt impressed his first gaping audiences as a man who was likely to lead them to victory.

I have not heard whether the German air force today exhibits the same symptoms of an inner awareness of inferiority.

The difference in the equipment of the Royal Air Force and the Luftwaffe is in part due to the recent origin and rapid expansion of the latter. The time element was all-important for Germany and could never be lost sight of. This had cut short the time available for experiment and modifications of aircraft design in the light of experience and had encouraged rapid decisions and mass production. The Royal Air Force was encumbered with large numbers of different types of aircraft, including several thousand which were obsolete. It was also, oddly enough, hampered by the knowledge of improved types and new possibilities, by aircraft still on the drawing board, under construction, undergoing their first tests but still a long way from production.

In this case the French proverb was the truth: "*Le mieux est l'ennemi du bien.*" There is no doubt whatever that the Royal Air Force might have been im-

mensely stronger numerically at the outbreak of war
had a lower standard of quality been acceptable or even
if all the resources of the aircraft industry had been mobilized to produce standard types instead of a part of it
being occupied with adaptations and improvements of
existing types and with the design and testing of greatly
improved aircraft.

The result of the British determination to have nothing but the best was that few British factories were
capable of mass production of any types.

In the heart of hearts of the majority of Englishmen—or, at all events, of officers of the Royal Air Force
—the determination to secure only the best is not a
matter of practical policy alone but is something like a
moral principle which they would be ashamed to abandon.

Intellectually it is clear that whether it was the right
policy to pursue depended on the length of the war and
when it would occur. It would have been singularly
futile in 1939 to have been laying down plant for aircraft to be built in 1942 if we had been defeated like the
French in 1940. Yet matters on which there are such
deeply held, almost ethical, convictions can seldom be
decided by the intellect alone. Just as the defensive
policy imposed on the French army seems to have rotted
the will to victory and to have led to the defeat of
France, so a decision to give up aiming at perfection and

to take the second best would probably have done infinite harm to the spirit of the Royal Air Force and to the British aircraft industry.

The pilot of the Spitfire, and the latest fighter, the Typhoon, and the crew of the Wellington know that the best possible has been done for them when they are sent into the air. And they are determined to be worthy of the aircraft they love and trust.

Thanks to this instinctive policy, the best British fighters and bombers when the war broke out were greatly superior to the corresponding German types, particularly in regard to armament. So far there are no signs that the Royal Air Force will lose its qualitative superiority while there is some hope that with the help of the United States it will draw level with the Germans as regards numbers.

It is unnecessary for the reader to cram his mind with particulars of such obsolete models as Furys, Foxes, Harts, and Hinds, or with the Heinkel 60 or Henschel 123. But some familiarity with the principal British, German, and Italian aircraft is desirable if the accounts of air fighting in the later chapters are fully to be understood. Particulars are therefore given in an appendix which can be referred to as required.

A comparison of the relative strengths of the Royal Air Force and the Luftwaffe is a difficult matter. The facts are highly secret, and the figures can be easily altered by the inclusion or exclusion of obsolescent types on one side or the other.

A comparison of strengths must leave out "museum specimens," even though these may have their uses for particular jobs. Thus the German invasion of Holland was carried out by using as troop carriers air liners of the Luft Hansa, believed to be of no military value.

I have read in newspapers many figures giving the strength of the German air force today and contrasting them with the probable strength of the Royal Air Force. I shall not do that but I shall hazard my own guesswork figures of what the position was in April 1940—at the time when the Germans launched their attack on Norway.

1. *Fighters.*

British and French first-line strengths combined and German first-line strength were, I believe, about equal—between 1400 and 1500 aircraft.

The second-line fighter strength of the Luftwaffe was, I believe, between 2600 and 2700 aircraft, or more than a thousand stronger than the British and French reserve fighter strengths combined.

2. *Bombers.*

The German first-line strength was between 2400 and 2500 and, I believe, about 3½ times as strong as the British first-line strength. The German reserves were about 4500, which was, I believe, rather under 2½ times the British reserves of bombers.

Great Britain and Germany were, I think, almost equal as regards Coastal aircraft.

3. *Troop Carriers.*

Excluding obsolete slow machines and the fleet of Deutsche Luft Hansa, which played, in fact, a useful role in the invasion of Norway and of Holland, the Germans had some 1200 troop-carrying aircraft. These could, of course, be easily transformed into night bombers. Britain had virtually no troop-carrying aircraft.

The position when active air warfare began was soon made worse by the collapse of France. Moreover, by then the German numerical advantage was greater, since German production was greater. I cannot give figures for British aircraft production, but some indication of the position is obtained from the fact that in the winter of 1939–40 the Germans were said to be building at least seven Heinkels for every British Wellington.

The French Armée de l'Air had declined relatively to other countries in quality ever since 1918. The two worst evils of the modern industrial system, financial corruption and labour unrest, permeated the French aircraft industry and had rotted it. At the time when Germany was rearming on a vast scale the French people were dreaming of a Pacifist Internationalism of Labour and were enjoying a forty-hour working week.

The outbreak of war completed the ruin of the French aircraft industry. There was no intelligent system of reserved occupations, and general mobilization meant the calling up of all men of military age—not of young men only but of men in the reserve. A very large proportion of the skilled men in the aircraft industry, who were, in any case, all too few, were lost for good and all and remained with their regiments until the collapse of France.

The following figures are my guess at the approximate size of the Armée de l'Air just before the beginning of the German attack in the west.

Fighters. 1st line. 650	The Germans had between two and three times as many 1st line.
Reserve. 700	The Germans had between three and four times as many in their reserve.
Bombers. 1st line. 300	The Germans had six times as many 1st line.
Reserve. 100	The Germans had forty-five times as many in reserve.
Coastal. None.	

Except for the Curtiss fighters bought before the war in the United States, the aircraft with which the Armée de l'Air was equipped were markedly inferior in performance to corresponding types in both the Royal Air Force and the Luftwaffe.

By the beginning of April German aircraft production had certainly risen to fifteen hundred a month.

On the outbreak of war British aircraft production dropped sharply, and after six months of war was still below that of August 1939.

Some officers of the British Air Staff, with such figures in their minds, believed that nothing short of a miracle could save Britain and France from an appalling catastrophe which would be all the greater because it was absolutely unexpected by the public. Such officers were necessarily very few in numbers and suffered from the sensation that they were living in a vast lunatic asylum. The jubilant complacency of the public was natural and forgiveable, since there was, and still is, no censorship of the newspapers in the interests of truth. Any lie which magnified the strength of Britain and exaggerated the strength of the Royal Air Force might be printed and was readily believed.

It was hard for Air Staff officers to bear an equal complacency on the part of Naval and Army Staff officers who knew the elements of the position but regarded it as of no importance, since they were persuaded that aircraft were no good against ships or troops in trenches, as the case might be.

The months of respite which the German preparations had given the Allies were months of complacency and inertia, since the people had not been taken into the confidence of the government. And in a democracy it is impossible to apply compulsion or to put industry on a war footing unless the people realize the necessity for such measures.

The Chamberlain government had always been in that tragic dilemma which is so frequently revealed after the financial crash of a great company. They could not tell the country how near the brink of disaster it was for fear of precipitating that disaster. They never had been able to tell the public frankly what the position was, either before the war or after it was declared.

Not only had they been responsible for mistakes of judgment which the majority of British people had made with them, but they never faced the results of those mistakes or admitted them and had clung to power, hoping to remedy them, much as a financier hopes to restore the reserves which have been wasted.

It was important to conceal British weakness in aircraft and arms from the knowledge of the enemy. The government used this excuse to prevent criticism and to conceal the facts from Parliament and from leading public men. It was therefore only slowly that the truth about the relative strengths of Britain and of Germany in the air became known even to a small number of patriotic members of Parliament and those who are in the truest sense in a great democracy the servants of the public.

Yet nothing could be done until a clean breast of the position had been made, for just as insolvent company directors have to appeal to the shareholders for capital, so the British government had to appeal to every citizen of the British Empire, and to their cousins in the United States, and to all lovers of freedom throughout the world for the capital that every man is born with. They had to call up extra hours of work, sacrifice of pleasures and self-indulgences from many millions of men and women, and such a call would have been answered immediately the necessity was understood. It could not have been made by Mr. Chamberlain, however, without his resignation, and the gravest reflection which can be made on him is that, owing to his courage and tenacity and also to his deficiency of imagination, he was unable to foresee the disaster before it came. Honest and honourable, he was out of touch both with reality and with the possibilities of arousing the people.

The general state of mind of the British public during the months of waiting is indicated by the fact that the chief newspaper campaign on air matters was conducted by Lord Beaverbrook's newspapers, the *Daily Express* and the *Evening Standard*, in order to force the Air Ministry to relax the blackout regulations. The blackout was regarded as an unnecessary interference with retail trade, which suffered, owing to brilliantly illuminated window displays being forbidden. The idea that the less retail trade the better for the national economy and that every penny should be saved and lent to the government did not dawn on the public until it was forcibly awakened to our desperate needs by the defeat of France. By that time Lord Beaverbrook was Minister of Aircraft Production, and every little community in the British Empire was contributing to its Spitfire fund. Gratifying as such collections proved to the Chancellor of the Exchequer, all the money in the world could not hasten the output of Spitfires, which was governed by the number of jigs and the number of machine tools. Lack of imagination in a Prime Minister is expensive.

CHAPTER V

The Work of Coastal Command

AT THE OUTBREAK OF WAR Germany possessed about seventy submarines which immediately began to attack British and French ships and very soon extended operations to neutral shipping proceeding to British or French ports. Immediate countermeasures were taken by the Allied navies and by the Coastal Command of the Royal Air Force, acting in cooperation. All possible steps to hunt down and destroy enemy submarines had to be taken, and protection had to be given to shipping by the formation of convoys which were provided with naval escort and with air escort during the hours of daylight in all waters within two or three hundred miles of the British Isles.

Submarines are dependent on their electric batteries while submerged, and these have to be recharged while running on the surface. Thanks to the patrolling aircraft of the Coastal Command, it soon became dangerous for any enemy submarine to cruise upon the surface during daylight in the neighbourhood of Britain. In order to give Coastal Command aircraft a free hand their captains were kept informed of how many British and French submarines were out and of their whereabouts. They were thus free to attack any submarine outside these definite areas at sight.

In theory, a submarine caught upon the surface can defend itself from air attack with its gun. In practice, submarines submerge as fast as they can, which means that the gun crew have to go below the moment an aircraft is sighted. Cases have occurred in which submarines have "crash-dived" before the conning tower hatchway has been properly closed. There have been many cases in which aircraft of the Coastal Command have stalked enemy submarines under cover of cloud in order to get near enough to them without detection to attack successfully.

The steel hull of a submarine is very tough, and direct hits from powerful bombs or depth charges are usually needed to knock a hole in it. Thus in the majority of cases in which submarines have been bombed by aircraft they have escaped, though not without damage. In many cases all the lights on board have been put out; in other cases doors and hatchways have been jammed; in quite a number of cases bombing has resulted in the submarine springing a leak, and there has been time for the submarine to surface and for the crew to be rescued and taken prisoner by British naval forces called up by the aircraft. Direct hits from bombs have been seen to blow off the bows or the conning tower, and the U-boat has sunk with all hands.

The German submarines were equipped to stay out for considerable periods—two months or longer—and it was not safe for them to transmit wireless signals at regular intervals. The German Admiralty were therefore seldom in a position to know of their own submarine losses until U-boats had to be presumed lost, owing to being overdue. The British Admiralty and Air Ministry therefore took particular pains to keep their successes against submarines secret. This was important, since the U-boats did not cruise haphazard but lay in wait for their prey in certain very favourable areas. Owing to the admiralty policy of secrecy, the Germans were not aware of the need to send out another boat to replace one which had been lost. Thus particularly important areas were often free of submarines for some weeks.

It would be untrue to claim that the defeat of the first phase of the submarine attack was due to Coastal Command. Nevertheless, the first phase was defeated during the autumn and winter months. In the first week of the war thirty-five German submarines—that is almost exactly half the German fleet—were sighted by aircraft of Coastal Command, and about half of these were attacked.

The falling off in tonnage sunk was very largely due to the institution of the convoy system, and the safety of convoys was shared between the warships of the Royal Navy and the air escort provided during the hours of daylight by Coastal Command.

The following figures give a conception of the magnitude of the work of Coastal Command during the first year of the war. Thirteen million miles were flown in one hundred and six thousand flying hours. One hundred and sixty attacks were made on enemy submarines, and air escorts were provided for over fifty thousand ships in convoy.

As the convoy system was organized greater and greater demands were made on Coastal Command aircraft for escort duty. Convoys would be met several hundreds of miles out in the Atlantic by our great Sunderland flying boats which would fly round and round throughout the hours of daylight. Such duty meant taking off from the home base some hours before dawn and returning to it after dark, facing the wildest weather of the year and the intense strain of flying and keeping a lookout for many hours at a stretch. Sunderland flying boats were not at that time fitted with the automatic pilot, and the strain on the captain, who frequently preferred to be at the wheel himself, except when he knocked off for lunch, was very great indeed.

Lunch, by the way, is cooked on board by a couple of aircraftmen. Not all visitors feel inclined for it if the weather is rough, and out in the Atlantic it usually is rough during the winter months. In bad weather a Sunderland crashes and jars through the bumps, for all the world like a nightmare express train jumping the points in an unending sequence. One feels as though that bad dream we all have of falling and starting up with a violent shock had become the routine incident of waking life. Airsickness in such conditions is the rule until the crew has become acclimatized. Flying for many hours at a stretch out of sight of land demands navigation of a very high order. The Sunderland cannot exchange wireless signals with the convoy it is to meet or with its naval escort, which have to maintain wireless silence. The position of the convoy is only known approximately, and to pick it up in conditions of bad visibility by the first crack of dawn is by no means an easy task. Yet so good is the navigation of the young officers of Coastal Command that a flying boat which has been out on patrol in bad weather, out of sight of land, and receiving no wireless "fixes" for seven or eight hours has been able to fly straight to the spot where a ship that had sent out a wireless call for help was being attacked by a submarine on the surface and to sink the U-boat.

Though the safety of such an aircraft is chiefly dependent on her captain and crew, much depends on those at the base. The group captain there has to rely on his meteorological information and on his intelligent and imaginative understanding of what it will mean. Should the harbour or sheltered waterway which is the flying boat's anchorage be enveloped in *fog*, there can be little hope of a safe return. When fog comes in and settles down all the aircraft out must be diverted to another base, where conditions are better, in time for them to reach it in safety. Such considerations are equally important for those in command at bomber and fighter stations, but it is stressed here because fog is peculiarly liable to come in from sea and to lie over water. The commander of a flying-boat station thinks about fog all the time.

Another preoccupation shared by the commanders of every Royal Air Force station is that of the maintenance of enough aircraft to meet the urgent demands on them. An aero engine can only run some hundreds of hours before overhaul. This takes a certain number of hours. And it is not the engines only which need maintenance. Thus a certain proportion of the available aircraft are always hauled up on land, undergoing necessary repair. In an ideally run station that proportion would always be the same and there would be a fixed proportion of the aircraft ready for service. In flying-boat squadrons, in which the number of aircraft is only a third of what it is in fighter squadrons, the problem of maintenance needs more thought and skill. That is why it is mentioned here.

The work of the great Sunderland flying boats lies in the western approaches, around Ireland, for the west coast of Ireland presents many possible points of call for U-boats in urgent need of water, food, fuel, or communication with enemy agents. And from the North of Ireland up to the arctic circle and Iceland is also their beat.

Thus anywhere between Iceland in the North and Spain in the South a Sunderland may be on the watch.

It was extremely fortunate for Coastal Command that some time before war broke out the commonwealth government of Australia had selected the Sunderland for coastal patrol along the Great Barrier Reef, where Japanese vessels have often poached on the Australian pearl fisheries and for similar work. A number of Sunderlands built to their order were nearing completion, and a squadron of the Royal Australian Air Force was undergoing training in Britain in order to fly the boats back. All these aircraft and their officers and men were immediately placed at the disposal of the home government and made a most important addition to the strength of Coastal Command. These officers were the first wearing a Dominion uniform to take an active part in the air war.

Sunderland flying boats have been responsible for many rescues. The crews of torpedoed vessels of our own merchant marine, of neutral vessels, the survivors from enemy submarines, stray seamen who had been clinging many days and nights to rafts washed by the icy waters—many such have first known that they were saved from hearing the roar of engines and seeing the giant aircraft dipping down from the clouds and circling about them.

After the *City of Benares*, with its load of children who were being sent for safety to America, had been torpedoed and the survivors in the boats lay worn out, famished, and half conscious a small boy in one of the boats recognized a Sunderland and stood up and waved, and those in the flying boat saw his action and knew that their search had not been in vain.

I shall not tell again the spectacular story of the rescue of the entire crew of the S.S. *Kensington Court*, of thirty-four men by a Sunderland which alighted on the calm sea and took the men in from their boats as they were pulling away from their ship. For this the captain of the aircraft was given the Distinguished Flying Cross, and his name became known all over the British

Empire. I refer to it only to tell a sequel. While the world was still ringing with the story of the *Kensington Court* another Sunderland flying boat came across another sinking ship, with its boats pulling away from it. To some officers it might have seemed that the chance of fame had come, that there was a D.F.C. easily within his grasp. But that was not the way this anonymous officer looked at it. There was a bit of a swell, and, though not dangerous, it was not the kind of sea for which a Sunderland is built. It was clear also that the survivors in their boats were in no immediate danger. So the young captain reported his discovery, asked for naval assistance, and stood by until a destroyer came in sight to pick up the men in the boats. Then he went on with his patrol. That young flying-boat captain, in my opinion, really did better than the first man. But it is fitting that he should remain anonymous—he is so much the type of Coastal Command officer.

On more than one occasion a Sunderland flying boat has been attacked by numbers of enemy aircraft and has come out of the engagement almost undamaged after shooting down one after another of the attacking aircraft.

But for the narrow seas Sunderlands are not needed. They are ocean-going craft.

They have, however, proved of the very greatest value in the Mediterranean, where a recent feat has been the rescue of large numbers of British forces during the evacuation of Greece. On several trips we are told Sunderlands took off seventy of our troops at a time and on one occasion eighty-five, including the Sunderland's own crew. During this work they were working after dark, without lights or fighter protection. Incidentally, eighty-five men must weigh round about six tons.

There are many sorts of aircraft patrolling the coasts of Britain. One submarine, off the Mersey, was sighted twice in one day, on the first occasion by a Moth Light airplane which, being unarmed, was unable to attack the enemy but which was able to call up reinforcements. In the Channel the Avro Anson has done much of the patrolling work needed. The Ansons carried out routine anti-submarine patrols and also convoy work, taking the northward- and southward-bound east-coast convoys up and down the coast inside the mine fields. These convoys have naturally been the easiest marks for enemy air attack, and the work of their air escorts has been from the first as much to look out for mines and aircraft as for enemy submarines.

In the very early days of the convoy system there were naval reserve and merchant-marine officers who could not distinguish enemy aircraft from those of the Royal Air Force. Thus one morning the *Admiralty Summary of Naval Operations* contained a brief ac-

SUNDERLAND FLYING BOATS

The Short *Sunderland* long-range reconnaissance flying boat fitted
with four Bristol "Pegasus XXII" engines each of 820 h.p. Fitted with
multiple gun turrets fore and aft and two further gun positions in
the top of the fuselage she is a veritable "Battleship of the Air." With
her four engines developing a total of 3,360 h.p. at 6,250 ft. she
attains her maximum speed of 210 m.p.h. and has a range of approximately 2000 miles.

count of how an east-coast convoy had been shadowed for several hours by hostile aircraft but had kept them at a distance by steady anti-aircraft fire. The *Air Ministry Summary of Operations* told the same story from the angle of the Captain of the Fleet of Blenheims, ordered to provide the convoy with an escort:

"Owing to their persistent shelling, we kept out of range throughout the afternoon."

Oh dear! Oh dear! After that an air-liaison officer sailed with the senior naval officer of every escort.

That sad story is told, not as a reproach to the British navy, but to illustrate the fact that full understanding and cooperation between two services or two branches of the same service is not just a matter of good will. Experience and intimate knowledge is needed, and first-class staff work too. It does not spring into existence of itself. And, lacking the knowledge which would enable him to recognize a Blenheim aircraft, that officer of the reserve (one may presume he was elderly) did perfectly right in taking no chances with the damned newfangled things that drop bombs and torpedoes on honest seamen out of the sky.

Once in my life I have been out with hawk and hound—that is to say, on a grouse moor, with an Irish setter to put up the birds and a couple of Peregrine falcons to bring them down. There was excellent cooperation between hawk and hound, yet there was no love lost between them. Indeed, there was the deepest jealousy and dislike, without the slightest attempt at an understanding of each other's gifts. So I shall not compare the cooperation of British Coastal Command aircraft and destroyers to that of hawk and hound, for, whatever the occasional mistakes which arose in the early days, there was always the fullest sympathy and understanding of each other's work. This was helped by the fact that many senior officers of the Coastal Command had begun life in the Royal Navy and had retained close touch with their colleagues afloat. It was not only senior officers who had naval experience. For instance, one of the keenest and most valuable men belonging to the ground staff of a station of Coastal Command, a pilot officer of the R.A.F.V.R., is a retired rear admiral of the Royal Navy! He felt that the greatest use he could make of his naval experience was to help the young men of the Coastal Command. Thanks to men like him, there is none of the antagonism of hawk and hound, but the humorous understanding of an elder and younger brother who have embarked upon the same adventure.

Anti-submarine patrols and convoy escort form only a part of Coastal Command work. In the first ten months of the war these duties covered most of what was needed in the Channel and the western approaches, but in the North Sea it was particularly important from the first to keep a watch on the Norwegian coast, by which German ships often ran the British blockade, and the German North Sea coast, from which surface raiders and commerce destroyers stole forth.

Both these were the particular jobs undertaken by the Lockheed Hudson aircraft of Coastal Command. One of these searches was to find the German ship *Altmark* in which British seamen were being taken prisoner to Germany. The *Altmark* was located on February 16, 1940, by two Hudsons and then intercepted by our destroyers in a Norwegian fjord, and our seamen were rescued from a horrible captivity. Such sweeps and searches were, of course, usually combined with anti-submarine patrol, and, in addition, there was the always-present possibility of coming across enemy aircraft and of intercepting and engaging them.

The conditions of visibility are all-important for such patrols, and the area of sea visible to a reconnaissance aircraft under average conditions is so often exaggerated that the difficulty of the work is underestimated.

The area that patrolling aircraft can search for submarines, either submerged or on the surface, for enemy shipping, etc., depends more on visibility at sea than on the speed of the aircraft.

The first set of diagrams shows an area of sea 90 miles by about 225 miles. In good visibility (fifteen miles on either beam) three aircraft with a cruising speed of 225 m.p.h. could cover this area in an hour, the wind being neglected. But if visibility is bad (only three miles on either beam) as in Fig. 1B, the three aircraft can only search an area eighteen miles wide, leaving four fifths of the original area unsearched.

Fig. 1C shows what happens when the visibility varies. The three aircraft set out, flying thirty miles apart, in good visibility but encounter two patches of bad weather, so that the strips of sea that each aircraft is able to search are narrowed and a considerable area is left unsearched between them.

The second set of diagrams shows areas on the earth's surface that an aircraft at a height of one thousand feet is able to see under varying conditions.

It should be *geometrically* possible to see a distance of about forty-five miles from a height of one thousand feet. The area, of about 5,700 square miles, is shown in Fig. 2A.

In practice, however, visibility is only as much as thirteen miles, on an average of six to seven days a month, in the neighbourhood of the British Isles. In such conditions an area of about 640 square miles, as shown in Fig. 2B, is visible. Under such conditions the "feather" of the periscope of a moving submarine is not visible at a distance of more than four miles.

On thirteen to sixteen days a month visibility is about six to seven miles, as shown in Fig. 2C and an area of about 130 square miles is visible. On ten to twelve days

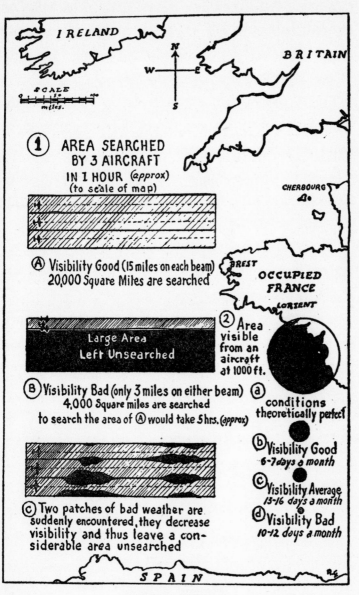

VISIBILITY DIAGRAM

a month visibility is only about three miles, as shown in Fig. 2D, and an area of about twenty-eight square miles is visible.

The above generalizations are true on the average. In winter, when hours of daylight are shorter and thick weather is experienced for weeks at a time, performance will be below what is shown, and search often becomes impossible. In fine summer weather conditions are better. The size of the object searched for is obviously another limitation which is not here considered.

As has been indicated, the first German attack on British and neutral shipping was almost completely mastered by the early months of 1940. A large proportion of German submarines was sunk, and many crews were captured. Germany, however, pushed ahead with submarine construction, and large numbers of the smaller type of boat were built and are being built now.

The defeat of France and occupation of the French Atlantic coast completely changed the whole position in favour of the Germans. Not only was the British navy deprived of the aid of all save a very few of the large fleet of French torpedo boats and submarine chasers, while its responsibilities were almost trebled by the entry of the numerically powerful Italian navy into the war, but the Germans were provided with ideal bases for their submarines. Before they had these bases the U-boats had to thread our mine fields and elude our vigilant patrols over the North Sea. To take up a position off the Scillies in the western approaches they had either to make an extremely hazardous voyage down the Channel and through the straits of Dover, a distance of seven or eight hundred miles, or they had to go north about round Scotland and the west coasts of Ireland, a safer route but double the distance.

From the French bases of Brest and Lorient the German submarines are only about 160 miles from the Scillies, and it is deep water all the way.

The Germans, moreover, have learned the lesson of the first months of the war. They know how extremely vulnerable submarines are to attack from the air. They therefore employ their submarines in cooperation with aircraft. These are chiefly of large long-range type—the Focke-Wulf Condor and Kurier, which are based at Merignac, just west of the city of Bordeaux. The new German tactics are for the aircraft to search the ocean for British convoys and report their position and direction to the German submarines. They also keep watch for and give warning of the patrols of our Coastal Command aircraft. When these German aircraft spot any vessels which have got out of convoy or are at some distance from naval or air escort they attack them.

Though the general run of German submarines is now smaller than those in commission at the outbreak of war, they are more numerous, far more efficiently placed, and better protected. They are no longer blind, because there are aircraft to see for them.

The British navy and Coastal Command have had to face an entirely different problem from the late summer of 1940 onwards, and one which would have been immeasurably more difficult but for the transfer of United States destroyers and revenue cutters to the British flag.

Coastal Command has been considerably increased and is likely to be greatly increased in the future. Both Coastal and Bomber Command aircraft have made continual raids on the submarine bases at Brest, Lorient and other places, as well as on the Merignac aerodrome.

Raids on the Focke-Wulf aircraft factories at Bremen and on the submarine construction yards and slipways at Kiel are another side of the same work—the battle of the Atlantic.

CHAPTER VI

Work of Bomber Command

IMMEDIATELY following the British declaration of war on Germany a large mixed force of bombers was sent to attack the German fleet lying off the western end of the Kiel Canal as Brunsbüttel and at Cuxhaven on the opposite side of the estuary of the Elbe. This was the "Kiel raid." It was carried out by Wellingtons, the latest type of British bomber, flying at low level in line astern, and by Blenheims. It proved expensive, and the results were incommensurate with the losses. The plain fact is that, since the British navy was immensely superior to the German and the German to the Royal Air Force, we had no Wellingtons to throw away. For propaganda purposes the Kiel raid was represented as a great British victory. So was the charge of the Light Brigade at Balaclava.

The lesson of the raid was one which neither the British nor the German Air Staff was willing to admit, and considerable numbers of aircraft were sacrificed by both sides in an effort to sink battleships with *bombs*. It has been abundantly proved that, lacking the element of surprise, the bomber stands little chance of success and that losses in the attacking aircraft will be high. Torpedo-carrying aircraft are another story.

The months of waiting—the "phony" war—held up all the carefully prepared British plans of a strategic offensive on German industry and communications. It was in the character of such an offensive that the British Air Staff was to show its brains, and before proceeding to describe in detail further activities of Bomber Command in the months of waiting it may be as well to compare British and German plans for the use of bomber aircraft.

As has been shown in the account of the invasion of Poland, the Germans planned to use their aircraft principally, if not entirely, during daylight for the following purposes:

Army cooperation and dive-bombing of the enemy's strong points and centres of resistance.

Attack on communications and aerodromes.

Bombing of the principal cities in order to inspire panic in the population.

Of these the most important function was that of army cooperation. When we consider the invasion of Holland and of Norway we shall see that the advance guard of the invading forces was to consist of air-borne parachutists who would seize aerodromes to which other air-borne troops would be brought in troop-carriers. Meanwhile the invasion proper would be carried out by mechanized forces and tanks whose movements would be directed from the air. Whenever these mechanized forces met with a serious defence which they could not outflank they would, in Air Marshal Sir Philip Joubert de la Ferté's phrase, "whistle up their air" and wait while the obstruction was flattened out by dive-bombing attacks.

No such intimate collaborations between air and ground forces had been planned, much less rehearsed, by the Royal Air Force and the British army before the war.

A curious paradox appears to have characterized the development of the Royal Air Force. On the one hand, every encouragement was given by its senior officers to every sort of scientific development, and wide powers had been given to the various advisory committees of scientists.

On the other hand, a strange conservatism, mental inertia, and lack of curiosity was shown with regard to tactical devices which had been developed abroad. This is particularly noticeable with regard to the dropping of parachute troops. For years parachutists had been dropped by the thousand in the Russian manoeuvres. But there can be little doubt that the British Air Staff disliked the idea and made no large-scale experiments of their own with parachutists. When in the Finnish war parachutists were dropped by the Russians the British Air Staff rejoiced that they had achieved little and convinced itself that the majority were shot down in the air. The success of German parachutists in Holland came as a shock to a deep-rooted prejudice. We have since been quick to acknowledge the mistake and to remedy the deficiency. The first British parachutists were dropped in South Italy in February 1941. The Germans will bitterly regret that they showed us the value of parachute troops, for our parachutists can be dropped in France, Belgium, Holland, and Norway, the populations of which hate the Germans and will do all they can to help our men achieve their missions and hide them afterwards.

Similarly, the Royal Air Force had made no large-scale experiments with towing heavy gliders loaded with troops or equipment or with troop-carrying aircraft.

The explanation, I believe, was not only that the Royal Air Force was an independent service and jealous of its independence and that the British army was not air-minded.

It was, to some extent, because there is no long-standing tradition of a great army in Britain. Indeed, the traditional role of the British army is of a small professional force capable of defending the bases of the British navy. Our navy has always been our offensive long-range arm, and when danger threatens abroad our instinctive reaction is to send a battleship and to wonder what the navy is doing about it. The British army is for police work in the Empire and for defence. It was therefore natural that the Royal Air Force should be regarded and look upon itself as a second navy.

All that the Air Staff, with few exceptions, appear to have envisaged was that they should provide a few army cooperation aircraft for artillery spotters and a few aircraft to carry generals about. And, in return, all they would expect of the army was to provide guards for aerodromes so as to relieve airmen, who are skilled men, of the drudgery of mounting guard.

But I think the real explanation of this attitude is that senior officers of the Royal Air Force who had served in the war of 1914–18 were, at all costs, determined to avoid the mistakes in the use of air power which had resulted from its being at the disposal of soldiers who used it merely for local and tactical purposes.

In the late summer of 1918, in face of opposition, a small independent air force had been created with Handley Page bombers capable of bombing Berlin. But before they could be used for that purpose the German armies collapsed, and the armistice was signed.

The whole British theory of the use of air power had grown up out of that might-have-been, reinforced by a horror of the holocaust of young pilots' lives thrown away in maintaining ascendancy in the air over the narrow strip of the enemy front line, where all his defences were concentrated.

The British Air Staff had studied the German armament industry and the whole interlocking industrial system in the greatest detail. They knew the weak links and where and how to attack them. They realized also the paralysis and lost time in factories which result over a widespread area whenever an alert is signalled. They had worked out plans to strangle Germany by paralyzing her war effort.

All such plans remained simply plans on paper, thanks to the unofficial truce which reigned until the German armament industry, working unmolested for nine months, had produced the weapons with which the German army was to break the Western front and overrun France, Belgium, and Holland in a few weeks. It was natural that the months of unofficial truce, when no bombing was allowed, should be used in perfecting the existing plans for the strategic offensive, in inventing new plans, and in rehearsing them. The first and most important thing was to train British bomber crews to find their way over Germany by night and to make certain that they could locate their future targets exactly. Thus an immense series of flights over Germany in the hours of darkness was inaugurated.

These essentially training flights were made use of to scatter many millions of leaflets in the German and Czech languages which aimed at encouraging those elements of the population critical of the Nazis and exciting disaffection in Germany.

The scale of these "leaflet raids" is shown by the fact that by the middle of March 1940 over fifty million leaflets had been scattered in Germany, Austria, Czechoslovakia, and Poland.

About the middle of March 1940 one of our longrange Whitley bombers lost its way on the return flight from Warsaw and landed in what the pilot believed to be a French field. Soon afterwards he saw soldiers coming up in German uniforms, so he took off again and afterwards made a safe landing in France. The advanced air bases in eastern France were of considerable use in affording alternative bases for these training flights to return to by night and in the photographic reconnaissances which were carried out by day. It became the practice, for example, to send out aircraft on photographic reconnaissance of important German industrial targets in the Ruhr and the Rhineland. These would take off from one of the advanced air bases in France and return via the German coast and the North Sea to Britain. Occasionally such a route ended in the infringement of Dutch or Belgian neutrality and in vigorous protests from the Dutch or Belgian governments. On one or two occasions British aircraft damaged by German fighters came down in neutral territory. But there were far more infringements of Belgian neutrality by German reconnaissance aircraft seeking to escape our patrols of Hurricanes in Flanders or to steal into France from the flank.

The results of these photographic reconnaissances over Germany were of the greatest value in future operations, and the photography of military and industrial targets was carried out on an enormous scale and from great heights by high-speed, practically invisible aircraft. An important part of the education of pilots and navigators was in the interpretation of photographs. In this way they were able to study German methods of camouflage, etc. Later on, after the strategic offensive had begun, photography both by day and night of the targets before and after bombing provided data of crucial importance. Indeed, the whole program had to be continually revised and altered in the light of photographic information.

ARMSTRONG WHITWORTH *WHITLEYS* BEING "BOMBED-UP"
FOR ACTION.

For it is chiefly by photographs that the actual damage done by our raids is assessed, and photographs of German repairs determine when another raid on the same area will be necessary.

The months of waiting were thus put to great use in training our bomber crews. There were few losses though our aircraft met with intense anti-aircraft fire. There is no doubt, however, that such losses were bitterly felt by the pilots and crews of Bomber Command at that time, simply because they were not hitting back at the enemy. A loss of an aircraft at that date seemed to one and all an aircraft thrown away for the sake of the wretched leaflets. Their attitude of mind was transformed immediately they carried bombs.

The winter of 1939–40 was an extremely hard one, and there were numbers of cases of frostbite among bomber crews. Owing to icing, some of our aircraft were lost, while others saved themselves by returning to bases in France instead of England or made forced landings over the French frontier.

The exceptionally hard winter caused far greater hardship in Germany than in England or France. It brought traffic on the Danube to a standstill and led to a breakdown on the overworked German railways. There was an acute coal shortage in most German cities which meant not only suffering to individuals but a slowing up of all war preparations. Indeed, it is probable that had the winter been one of ordinary mildness the invasion of the Low Countries and the attack on the Western front would have been launched at least a month and probably two months earlier. It is probable that in that case a German invasion of England would have occurred in the summer of 1940.

Owing to their very different strategical conceptions, the Germans did not send their bombers on night flights over Britain. We shall see the results of this lack of training in night flying later on.

In November 1939 Hitler made a speech which was of more interest than usual, owing to its containing the boast that Britain would be speedily defeated, thanks to a German secret weapon. Soon after this British ships began to blow up in shallow waters in circumstances which precluded their having been torpedoed or destroyed by mines laid from submarines. The "secret weapon" turned out to be a magnetic mine exploded by the variation of the magnetic field caused by the passage of a steel vessel above it. The construction of the magnetic mine was not long a secret, and the method of mine laying which started about the second or third week in' November was soon· afterwards observed by an officer taking a stroll round Dunkirk harbour on a clear night. He reported having seen two enemy seaplanes glide down silently, with their engines throttled back, at slow speed. When over the harbour, within a few feet of the water, each in turn had dropped a large object, and they had then opened up their engines and flown away up the Belgian coast.

Other enemy seaplanes were observed at night resting on the water, close inshore, and these were also shown to have been laying magnetic mines. For a short time the magnetic mine worked havoc, but it was for a very short time. Directly its construction was revealed several means were found to render it harmless. In the first place, the mines were exploded *in situ*. In the second, every British vessel as it came into port was fitted with a "de-gaussing" band which prevented it from setting up a disturbance in a magnetic field adjacent to it. Until these methods had been elaborated, and while they were being put into effect, the Royal Air Force endeavoured to deal with the trouble at its source. It was useless to attempt to intercept the mine-laying seaplanes of the Luftwaffe in the darkness once they had got into the air, but it was possible to bomb them on the water and prevent them taking off. The chief bases of the German seaplanes were only a few miles from the Danish mainland. Other bases were on the Frisian Islands of Borkum and Wangeroog, the scene of that wonderful book, *The Riddle of the Sands*, by Erskine Childers. Since the German seaplanes only laid mines during the hours of darkness, all that was needed was to prevent them from taking off from shortly before sunset until shortly after midnight. For this purpose Bomber Command instituted the "security patrol" over Sylt and other seaplane bases of the German air force.

Every evening one or two pairs of our bombers would arrive at Sylt and Borkum as dusk fell and cruise around the islands for a couple of hours. But before the first pairs left they would be relieved by other pairs which would, in turn, be relieved by third and, if necessary, fourth pairs. If the security patrol observed a light showing at the seaplane base or a flare path on the water they would come down to a low altitude and bomb or machine-gun the enemy. Naturally enough, the visiting aircraft were subjected to considerable anti-aircraft fire, but it did not prove effective, and German fighters seldom attempted night flying at this period. The results of the security patrol were to make it extremely difficult and often impossible for the mine-laying seaplanes to take off.

During these weeks of winter the weather had been becoming steadily colder and colder, and for some weeks the intense cold made the security patrol over Sylt and Borkum unnecessary. The estuaries of the German rivers and the shallow sea round the Frisian Islands became filled first with blocks of floating ice which made it impossible for a seaplane to take off or to alight on the water, for fear of knocking a hole in its floats, and later with actual pack ice which impeded the movements of the German fleet and of "Flak" anti-aircraft vessels.

Thanks to the security patrol and to the weather combined, Hitler's secret weapon proved a failure.

Besides the security patrol over Sylt and the air bases in the Frisian Islands, lasting from dusk until the early hours of the morning, Bomber Command carried out a considerable number of sweeps in Heligoland Bight by day.

These sweeps were part of the policy of seeking out and attacking German shipping, and a number of German destroyers met with were, in fact, attacked. The wisdom of this policy then was questionable, since in Heligoland Bight our bombers were not only exposed to the inevitable dangers which attend the bombing of warships but were doing so in the most dangerous possible area. They were flying into a bag. The consequence was that on several occasions our bombers were ambushed and attacked by immensely superior numbers of enemy fighters and had to fight their way out. It is true that they brought down numbers of enemy fighters, but on two or three of these occasions the British loss in bombers was high, and, in my opinion, such losses at that time were unjustifiable.

To have made the enemy pay as heavily as ourselves our men would have had to shoot down eight times as many Messerschmitt 109s as we lost Wellingtons. But,

even had that proportion been achieved, the loss of a
single Wellington should have been avoided. It weakened our strategic offensive before it began. Moreover,
at this time, remember, Germany was probably building more than seven Heinkel 111s for every Wellington.

The policy of carrying out offensive sweeps against
the German fleet in Heligoland Bight was repeating in a
less excusable form the mistake of maintaining "ascendancy in the air" by making our aircraft fly over the
German side of the front during the war of 1914–18.

One of these sweeps revealed a tragic mixture of unreality and error. A large force of Wellingtons was sent
to bomb the German fleet at sea. Unfortunately it was
in port. They located it but did not drop any bombs,
owing to the proximity of buildings on shore! The
German fighters were waiting for our bombers in
swarms, and there was a running fight which resulted
in our losing a large proportion of the aircraft we had
sent and in others being damaged. Although our losses
were high, they would have been higher still had it not
been for the magnificent discipline of our bomber
crews. Our aircraft kept formation and flew and fought
as a disciplined body. They closed up as each one was
knocked out, and so the survivors came home over the
North Sea after the German fighters no longer cared to
follow them.

In one of these sweeps a formation of three aircraft was sent off shortly after a formation of fifteen, on exactly the same course. The fifteen fought their way out of a difficult position. The three which followed were never heard of again.

One cannot help feeling that those responsible did not ask themselves: "Is Germany vulnerable on sea or on land? Will the loss of her fleet knock her out? Or is her oil supply and her overworked railway system a more vulnerable point? If the latter we must save every bomber for when we can attack her there."

Instead of such a decision we must surmise that exasperation with the waiting role imposed by Gamelin dictated these unprofitable operations, simply because they were the only ones in which Bomber Command could attack the enemy.

It is possible that in that fact lies their justification. The senior officers of the Royal Air Force have to concern themselves very closely with the state of mind of the men under their command. The psychology and morale of pilots and crews are all-important, and because they are fewer in number than the soldiers each individual counts more, and the whole question looms larger and can receive more attention. There is no doubt that the period of waiting was more trying to the pilots and crews of Bomber Command than to any airmen in the service.

Coastal Command pilots and crews were doing a big job of work and doing it well. Those of Fighter Command were training and were always alert for the enemy to come over. But the pilots and crews of Bomber Command were exposed to all the dangers they would meet with in real war but felt that it was "phony" in all other respects. They had to go out continually on hazardous night flights, facing ice, anti-aircraft fire and enemy fighters, and ground fog when they got back. Yet they felt themselves futile and had no assurance that they would ever be anything else. All the hours of training on the bombing ranges seemed wasted, since it turned out that real war was waged, not with bombs, but "bumf"— for such was the impolite way in which they spoke of Neville Chamberlain's oratory after it had been translated into the languages of Central Europe.

The conviction of futility is the dry rot of armies and it runs through almost all of them. It leaves men moulded into the shapes of discipline but it eats away initiative, self-respect, happiness in one's work, and the careless devilry of the fighting spirit.

Once the fungus of futility was allowed to eat into the Royal Air Force it would be all up with its offensive spirit. And it is difficult to keep up the offensive spirit in men who are not allowed to hit back. Thus it is possible that the senior officers may have felt that, at all costs, their pilots must be saved from futility and have sent them to have a crack at the German fleet. If events proved it futile, it was futility of a heroic sort.

One may sum up by saying that there were mistakes during the period of waiting. Nevertheless, much was achieved. The value of leaflet dropping can only be assessed after the war is over—if then—when we can obtain evidence on a large scale of its effects on the minds of the German working class and opponents of Nazi rule. The ordinary evidence which comes out of Germany, through journalists and neutral travellers, is not of the slightest value in such an estimation, for such informants reflect only the business community and the bourgeoisie. The leaflets are not aimed at them but at the inarticulate workman who is working longer hours and getting less food and who has a vague shamefaced belief in the brotherhood of man. It was never expected to bring about a revolution by means of leaflets. Who would be so foolish as to expect that? But if they lessened enthusiasm for the war and spread discontent and so slowed up German war production by a quarter of 1 per cent they would have been worth while. And the percentage might be much higher than that.

But the immense value of the training flights associated with leaflet dropping cannot be too much emphasized. By the spring of 1940 Bomber Command aircraft had the best night-flying pilots and the best navigators that the world had ever known. Their courage and their accuracy, when the time came, did much to offset the great advantages in numbers and geographical situation possessed by the enemy.

CHAPTER VII

Fighter Command and the B. A. F. F.

Beginning in october, the German air force made frequent attacks on the British fleet. If possible they surprised it when at anchor. Such were the attacks made first in the Firth of Forth and later at Scapa Flow.

At this period of the war the British navy intercepted all merchant shipping proceeding to North European ports and frequently sent it to be searched for contraband at Lerwick, the chief port of Shetland, which in normal times is the base of a fleet of herring drifters. Lerwick harbour soon became packed with shipping of all nationalities and formed an ideal target for Nazi bombers. There were also numbers of British flying boats based on the Shetlands, where the voes provide magnificent stretches of sheltered water.

As it slowly dawned on the Germans that the initial submarine attack had failed they made determined efforts to drive British shipping out of the North Sea by other means. Raiding aircraft were instructed to attack everything afloat and did not hesitate to machine-gun light vessels and the smallest fishing boats. As we have seen, merchant shipping was at once formed into convoys which were given naval and air escort, and steps were taken to arm all British ships. Owing to the shortage of anti-aircraft guns, it was some time before the vessels of the fishing fleet could be armed. The first arms the fishermen obtained were rifles and several claims were made by stouthearted skippers to have brought down a German bomber with a rifle bullet.

While these attacks were going on up and down the coast the chief—indeed, the only—adequate protection of our shipping was that given by patrolling fighter aircraft and the aircraft of Coastal Command.

During one of the raids on the British fleet at anchor in the Firth of Forth H. M. cruiser *Southampton* was hit by a bomb which exploded in the water, doing little damage, and the destroyer *Mohawk* was also hit.

The "phony" or artificial nature of the war at this time is shown by the fact that captured German pilots revealed they had strict orders to avoid any damage to the Forth Bridge!

The German raiders on that occasion were inter-

SPITFIRES ABOVE THE CLOUDS

The Supermarine *Spitfire*, single-seat day and night fighter, supreme among fighter aircraft throughout the world. She carries eight machine guns mounted in the wings, four each side of the fuselage. The official maximum speed is 367 m.p.h. at 18,400 ft.

cepted by Spitfires, and four were shot down by the pilots of an auxiliary squadron, which has since distinguished itself greatly.

At Scapa and in the Shetlands the German raiders were more fortunate, since none of our Spitfire or Hurricane squadrons were based on the Orkneys or the Shetlands, and the Gladiators sent up were slower than the raiders they were to intercept. The first bombs actually dropped on land by the Germans in Britain fell in the Shetlands, not far from Lerwick, and killed a rabbit. Shortly afterwards a civilian was killed by a bomb dropped on the Orkneys. And from these precedents the permissible bombing objectives slowly spread from ships to the fauna of small islands and from them to the inhabitants of the mainland. The Royal Air Force bombed the air base on the island of Sylt at a date when they would not have bombed a similar base on the mainland.

The only large-scale offensive operation carried out by aircraft of Fighter Command during the early months of the war took place on the twenty-ninth of November 1939. It was a low-level attack by Blenheims on the mine-laying seaplane base at Borkum and was strikingly successful.

Our aircraft took the enemy completely by surprise and came over so low that a German standing on one of the hangar roofs was seen to fall off, either from fear or from excitement, for he had not been shot at. Our air-craft sprayed the slipways, the aircraft drawn up upon them, and seaplanes riding at anchor, with streams of machine-gun bullets. They damaged several enemy air-craft severely, most probably beyond repair. All our aircraft returned safely. The success of this raid was in striking contrast to some of the sweeps of Bomber Command aircraft in this area which have already been described. The bomber sweeps had obviously been ex-pected to arrive at the precise time when they did. There were dozens of German fighters up already, waiting to intercept them some way off the German coast. The Fighter Command raid, on the other hand, caught the Germans completely unprepared.

Communications with Germany, I am told, were by no means difficult in the early months of the war. Tele-phone communication between Britain and Northern Ireland and between Northern Ireland and Eire was rapid. There was a German consulate working at full blast in Dublin, and telegrams from Eire to Germany via the U.S.A. were rapid.

I believe—indeed, it is notorious—that there were numbers of German agents of all descriptions at large in Britain at that time. There were the usual professional spies; there were bogus refugees from Nazi tyranny; there were genuine refugees whose loyalty to Germany proved greater than their gratitude to the country which had offered them hospitality; there were refugees who were trying to re-establish themselves with the Nazis; there were British Fascists, and Irish Sinn Feiners, and Irish labourers who had been bribed by German agents in Eire. By a strange absence of imagination, almost every important British aerodrome was originally laid out alongside a main road—never at the end of a private road of its own. I only know of one important British aerodrome in the early days which did not have to conduct all its movements of aircraft in the full glare of publicity. Every other aerodrome I have visited was watched by dozens of small boys and idlers and passersby, and it is a safe bet that there was always a German agent among the watching crowd.

There is a lot to report besides the actual arrivals and departures of aircraft by air. There are the numbers brought out from the hangars in the morning, the numbers undergoing overhaul and maintenance, the numbers dispersed along the edges of the aerodrome, and their precise positions.

Until the invasion of Holland the only authentic stories I heard of enemy agents in Britain were of attacks during the blackout hours in London on staff officers and civil servants who were believed to be carrying important papers. These attacks were probably the work of Fifth Column British Fascists in German pay. After the invasion of Holland the spy stories were everywhere, and most of them were ridiculously improbable.

It is perhaps worth mentioning that throughout the autumn and winter months there were practically no German reconnaissance flights to any depth inland over the British Isles either by night or by day.

Though interceptions of enemy aircraft were few and far between during this period, much was learned about the performance of British fighter aircraft and the tactics of air fighting.

The installation of a cine-camera synchronized with the machine guns so that photographs are taken automatically when the guns are fired has proved invaluable. After each combat the pilot is able to study a detailed film showing where his bullets went and what mistakes he made. Not only can he see which of his bursts registered on the target and which went wide but he can see how wide they went and can obtain an indication of where the enemy's fire went also.

The superiority of our eight-gun fighters did not prevent further experiment in armament, and a number of our fighter aircraft were armed with cannon after the style of the Messerschmitt 110. The drawbacks of the cannon would appear to be that fire cannot be continuous, or even rapid, and that the weight of the shells greatly limits the number of rounds which can be carried. Its advantages are in the longer range and the destructive action of the shell if a hit is registered. On the face of it one would judge that the cannon was a weapon most useful to the aircraft stalking, or ambushing an unsuspecting enemy, and that machine guns were likely to be handier in a dogfight in which a number of aircraft are engaged. I should expect cannon to be most useful for night fighters, particularly if mounted in a turret. I do not know whether they have been employed in this way or not.

From September 1939 until the end of the year the British air forces in France were not a separate command but consisted of an air component attached to the British Expeditionary Force under the orders of its commander in chief and of the Advanced Air Striking Force under those of Bomber Command.

The air component of the B.E.F. consisted of squadrons of fighters (Hurricanes), army cooperation (Lysanders), and bomber reconnaissance (Blenheims).

The A.A.S.F. consisted, in the first place, entirely of short-range Fairey battle light bombers. In December the British air forces in France were raised to the position of a separate command under Air Marshal Barratt, and both air component and the A.A.S.F. were increased by the addition of several squadrons of fighters.

As has been explained in Chapter II, all proposals made by Air Marshal Barratt or by the Air Ministry to bomb objectives in Germany were vetoed by the Allied commander in chief on grounds of general policy and for fear of German retaliation. General Gamelin even vetoed the bombing of objectives in Germany after the violation of the frontiers of Belgium and Holland!

Idleness almost always has a bad effect upon the morale of troops and is likely to be particularly danger- ous when they are forced to endure the discomforts of war conditions and are billeted in a foreign country. Our men were inevitably kept standing about for three months of one of the coldest winters Europe has ever known. It was here that the high level of intelligence and education and the *seriousness* of the airmen of the Royal Air Force was to stand them in good stead.

Training on the scale carried out by Bomber and Fighter Commands in Britain would have been the best remedy but it was made difficult by hampering restric- tions by the French. For some time they vetoed night flying, and the only bombing ranges available were in distant parts of France. Our aircraft were also, for the most part, kept standing in the open and were often covered with snow.

There was a shortage of aerodromes, and this was so great that the R.A.F. acquired sites and began to con- struct aerodromes of their own to the rear of their ad- vanced bases. This farsighted step turned out to be ex- tremely fortunate, since, though these aerodromes were not completed, they were in a sufficiently forward state to be of invaluable service when the battle in May began.

It was also fortunate that the French were induced to rescind their ban on night flying and that the battle squadrons could receive training in this.

CHAPTER VIII

The Air War in Norway

Access to Norway and Sweden was essential during the first phase of the war for the German production of munitions. The richest iron deposits in Europe are at Gellivare and Kiruna in the north of Sweden. A railway connects the iron mines with the port of Lulea on the Gulf of Bothnia and with Narvik in the north of Norway.

In the first seven months of 1939 Sweden supplied 45 per cent of Germany's iron-ore imports, which, on account of the richness of the ore, amounted to 50 per cent of Germany's iron imports. With the outbreak of war imports from Spain, France and other sources came to an end, and in the later months of 1939 imports from Norway and Sweden amounted to 88 per cent of Germany's imports of iron ore.

The cheapest pig iron in Europe is that produced from Swedish ore in the Ruhr blast furnaces. The most expensive is that produced at the Hermann Goering steelworks at Salzgitter, since the low-grade German ores require two or three times the quantity of coke for smelting.

The port of Lulea is icebound in winter and in the exceptionally severe winter of the first year of the war was icebound for longer than usual. German supplies had therefore to be shipped from Narvik. By hugging the coast of Norway it is possible for steamers to remain within Norwegian territorial waters until they can cross the Kattegat and follow the coast of Jutland down to the mouth of the Elbe.

If they could have cut off these supplies of Swedish iron ore the Allies would have almost crippled the German armaments industry. The importance of supplies of Swedish ore, and of Narvik, disappeared after the battle of France and the German occupation of the French iron mines in Lorraine.

In Scandinavia hatred and fear of Russia swung public opinion also against Germany, Russia's partner in aggression. And, had the Finns continued resistance after their front had begun to crumble and had the Russians pushed on to the objective of a port on the Atlantic, there is no doubt that Norway and Sweden would have welcomed an Allied expeditionary force which would have checked Russia and have secured the Baltic as a base from which to raid Germany.

All such plans ignored the immensely superior military strength of the German army and air force. They were excellent plans on paper but they were at least two years too soon. The lesson of the destruction of Poland had not been learned. It must also be remembered that, timid and cautious as they were, the Norwegians and Swedes were not in a position to gauge the weakness of the Allies.

While the Allied staffs were indulging in dream fantasies of amphibious warfare in the Baltic their opposite numbers in Germany were more practically engaged in giving their troops embarkation and disembarkation exercises on the Baltic coast. They already had detailed plans for the seizure of Norway in conjunction with a small body of Norwegian traitors headed by Major Quisling.

The occupation of Norway would bring Germany the following advantages:

1. It would forestall Allied occupation at the invitation of the Norwegian government and prevent an Allied threat to Germany's flank while she was making her attack in the West.
2. It would secure the Swedish iron-ore supply.
3. It would provide submarine and air bases for attacks on shipping in the North Sea, North Atlantic, and Scotland.

4. It would greatly increase the difficulties of the British navy in maintaining an effective blockade. German blockade runners and commerce raiders could shelter in north Norwegian harbours and fjords.

5. Germany could plunder Norwegian stocks of oil fuel, rubber, cotton, foodstuffs, etc., and could secure the entire Norwegian supply of fish and fish oil.

The coup was planned to be combined with the invasion and occupation of Denmark which was easy to carry out and unlikely to meet with resistance. Though on a smaller scale than the invasion of Poland, the invasion of Norway and Denmark was a more remarkable piece of staff work, and the coordination of the German land, air, and naval forces showed that the careful and painstaking military genius of the old German army had been inspired with a new boldness and originality derived from Nazi experience in conspiracy and revolt.

On April 9 the Germans invaded and occupied Denmark and invaded Norway, seizing Oslo, its capital and principal city. A German transport was sunk, but others were successfully run in. The German advance guard came in a stream of three hundred troop-carrying aircraft which landed on and immediately seized the principal Norwegian aerodromes. Stavanger and Bergen were taken with great rapidity, and very soon the German columns had pushed north and captured Trondheim. They did at least meet with resistance from the surprised and scattered Norwegian forces led by their gallant and honourable King. But Norway could not hold up the German advance without Allied help on a great and well-organized scale. The war of waiting, though still maintained in France, was nearing its end.

Aircraft of Bomber and Coastal Command made repeated attacks on German aerodromes and ships off the Norwegian and Danish coasts. Bergen, Stavanger, Trondheim, Kristiansund and Fornebu aerodromes in Norway were continually bombed, and so were those at Aalborg and Rye in Denmark and at Westerland on Sylt. But the Germans were in overpowering force and were using it, and, though their losses must have been higher than we knew at the time, our bombing made no difference to the result of the campaign and did not ever check it.

Meanwhile a hastily collected, ill-equipped Allied expeditionary force was landed at Namsos in an effort to recapture Trondheim. It could do little, for the Germans, as in Poland, had absolute command of the air, and the Allied forces could not make a movement which was not immediately reported. Moreover, they were heavily bombed.

The air protection for the Allied force consisted of aircraft of the Fleet Air Arm and of one squadron of Gladiator biplanes—eighteen aircraft. The story of this squadron was first told by Mr. Churchill and has often been told since, and I shall not enter into great detail. The aircraft were flown off an aircraft carrier in a snowstorm but landed safely on a hastily improvised landing ground on a frozen lake at Aandalsnes. Nothing had been cleared but the runway, and there was no shelter on the ground. The pilots had to stand about in the snow, without any protection against bombs and machine guns. They had to refuel and rearm their own aircraft, since there was practically no ground staff. On the first day German attacks with some ninety bombers lasted for over twelve hours. During this time the British pilots had continual combats with the enemy. At the end of the day only five Gladiators were serviceable. At the end of the second day only one Gladiator remained.

The following narrative by an officer of the Fleet Air Arm records one of those peculiar situations which occasionally arise in the odd conditions of modern war and which remind one more forcibly than any pacifist theory that war is an anachronism which has been forced on us.

"At approximately 1 P.M., April 27, I took off with two other aircraft in company. On reaching the coast near Molde, I saw H-A bursts in the sky in the direction of Aandalsnes. We proceeded in that direction at full speed at about twelve thousand feet and found a Heinkel 111 preparing to bomb H.M.S. *Flamingo,* which was lying off the town. The Heinkel was a thousand feet above us. As we climbed towards it it dropped a salvo of bombs which missed ahead and then made off towards the south. The enemy had a two-mile lead, owing to her superior height, but after a few minutes at full throttle I managed to get within range. His rear gunner opened fire on me at six hundred yards, but I did not reply until I judged I was four hundred yards astern of him, when I opened fire with a long burst which appeared to kill his rear gunner. By this time my number two had caught up and was attacking him from underneath while I was attacking him from above and from both beams. As soon as my ammunition gave out I manoeuvred in an attempt to allow my observer, whom I will call Smith, to have a shot at him. However, as my number three had now arrived on the scene and the enemy aircraft appeared to be losing height, with black smoke coming from his port engine, I drew away from the fight.

"Suddenly, however, without warning my engine quietly petered out, but, as I was at eleven thousand feet, I had plenty of time to look around and select a place for a forced landing. The chase and fight had lasted about fifteen minutes and had taken us in a south-southwesterly direction. Neither I nor my observer had any accurate idea of our position. Below there seemed to be nothing but snow and mountains, with no sign of any habitation. When we had glided down to five thousand feet we both spotted what appeared to be a road running along the side of a frozen lake with a few small houses at one end of it, so I decided to land there with my wheels up.

"We made a successful landing, and the other two machines circled round us until they were certain that we were unhurt. Then they made off. Not knowing how close we were to enemy lines, we set fire to our aircraft and, with the few belongings we had collected, started to make our way towards the road. Unfortunately the road was covered with anything from four to six feet of soft snow. It was practically impassable, but we found going on the lake itself was easier, although we were often waist-high in snow. It took us from 2:10 P.M., when we landed, until 4:30 to reach the houses we had seen from the air and which were not more than two miles away.

"They turned out to be wooden shacks, and in one of the three we found some rough beds, a stove, and wood, a primus stove, some dirty cooking utensils, matches, and a large bag of oatmeal. As we were exhausted after our struggle through the snow, we decided to spend the night there and review the situation the following day.

"We got both stoves going, made some very fine porridge, and had a good meal. Then we studied the map but could not fix our position within twenty miles. At about 6:15 we heard a whistle being blown and immediately jumped to the conclusion that a Norwegian ski patrol had found us but, on going outside, we saw a figure in grey uniform about two hundred yards away. Leaving Smith at the hut, I went towards the stranger and when I got near was not a little disturbed to find that his uniform had German eagles on the collar and that he had a large revolver at his waist and that he appeared to be asking me in German whether or not I was *Deutsch*. He could speak no English, and I could speak no German, but I managed to understand that he had two friends coming along, and, as neither Smith nor I were armed, the situation was becoming rather tricky. His two friends then arrived, also both armed, and they all insisted on shaking hands. Smith and I then asked them into our hut. One of them, the pilot, was an officer, while the other two were apparently members of his crew, so we assumed that they came from a German aircraft which must have been brought down in the vicinity. All three were very friendly and although they must have known that we were unarmed they did not threaten us in any way. The language problem was difficult, but we managed to understand that they had been shot down by three British fighters soon after 2 P.M. Then it began to dawn on Smith and myself that

they must be the crew of the Heinkel which we had
been attacking.

"The pilot appeared to be considerably upset because
his rear gunner had been killed, and when he asked us
what we were doing Smith and I exchanged quick
glances and said that we had been in an aircraft which
had forced-landed, owing to engine trouble. Luckily
he accepted this statement. One of the crew, too, had
a bullet through his elbow and was in considerable pain.

"Before the Germans arrived we had observed another building about a mile away which looked to be
quite large and well preserved. Giving the excuse that
I was going to search for more food, I set off for this
building, hoping to find somebody there, while Smith
remained at the hut. On my way I came across a sign-
post, and the name written up in large letters gave us
our position exactly. My objective turned out to be a
wooden hotel which had been bombed and obviously
deserted in a hurry. However, there was plenty of food
there, with beds and bedding and a telephone which I
could not get to work. I found my way back to the hut,
carrying a large tin of biscuits, and made the Germans
understand that Smith and I were going to spend the
night at the new residence while they could remain at
the old one. I think they realized that they were well
within Norwegian occupied territory, and they appeared to have no objection to this plan. We left them

the tin of biscuits for which the pilot insisted on giving me a packet of cigarettes from their emergency rations, and Smith and I arrived at the hotel shortly before 9 P.M., when it was beginning to get dark. We made some coffee on an oilstove and had a meal of biscuits selected from at least a dozen different tins. At 11 P.M. we retired to bed in the best double room, with plenty of warm feather bedding, as it was getting very cold. We turned out at 8 A.M. and had breakfast off bacon and eggs cooked in most professional style by myself, Smith making the coffee!

"After breakfast we talked the situation over and decided that the nearest point of civilization was twenty miles away and that it was out of the question to try and get there without skis. The telephone was out of action, as one of the lines had been destroyed by the bombing. There were several outhouses to the hotel, however, and I decided to search these in the hopes of finding some solution to the problem. This took a long time, as the doors were all snowed up, but eventually I did find one very ancient pair of skis.

"In the meantime, Smith, with the aid of his glasses, had discovered another group of buildings two or three miles away from the hotel which we decided we must investigate. At this moment, however, the Germans arrived on the scene and seemed quite prepared to settle down at the hotel with us, so we came to the conclusion that one of us must ski to the new collection of buildings we had spotted. Smith had never been on skis in his life, and, as I could boast of one trip to Switzerland some ten years ago, it was arranged that I should go. Unfortunately the German pilot insisted that one of his crew should accompany me, and we did not feel in a position to argue. In spite of numerous troubles I managed to outpace the German who was floundering through the snow and after I had gone about half a mile I had outdistanced him by about two hundred yards. At this point a Norwegian ski patrol, dressed in white, appeared as if from nowhere, halted us, and covered us with rifles. I was made to take off my skis and stood there proclaiming loudly I was English. Unfortunately the German also decided to say he was English, and after a few moments two shots rang out, and he dropped dead. (The Norwegians afterwards stated that he tried to draw his pistol.) The other shot just missed me but certainly gave me a scare! Two or three of the Norwegians then came up and searched me in no uncertain manner. The only thing I had on me which made them at all doubtful whether or not I was German was a 2/- piece with the head of George V on it. Smith, having heard the shooting, now came floundering through the snow to see what was happening and was in grave danger of being shot until I shouted to him to hold his hands up and not to move. He was also searched, and

I managed to make one of the Norwegians understand that there were two Germans at the hotel armed with pistols. They captured the two remaining Germans, who offered no resistance, and we were taken back to the hotel where there was a Norwegian who could speak fair English, and our nationality was more or less established.

"We were each lent skiing boots and a pair of skis and escorted to the group of huts I had originally been making for, which turned out to be one of the rendez-vous or headquarters of these ski patrols. There we found three nurses of the Norwegian Red Cross who had been retreating across country on skis from Oslo since the war began. All three girls spoke English, one very well indeed, having a Scots mother and having lived in Edinburgh most of her life. Our nationality was now definitely established, and were well looked after and most kindly treated.

"The officer in charge of the patrol made arrange-ments for an escort to take us and the members of the Red Cross over the mountains to Stryne that night, as anybody moving by day was liable to be machine-gunned from the air. Indeed, while the Norwegians were searching us a Heinkel had machine-gunned us from about four thousand feet and had dropped bombs at the hotel, all without effect. Unfortunately the escort did not turn up, so it was decided to move without them, the party consisting of Smith and myself, the three nurses and two doctors, and what appeared to be a couple of young local Norwegians. All were on skis except the two of us, but, as the crust of the snow froze hard at night, we were confident of being able to walk the twenty-one miles to Stryne. Shortly after 2 A.M. we set out and had an uneventful journey, arriving at about 7:30. At Stryne one of the local inhabitants gave us a very fine and welcome breakfast at his house, and we were sent on from there by bus to Nordfjordeid, where there was a Norwegian military headquarters. After a few hours there Smith and I were sent on by car and motorboat to Aalesund, where we arrived at 1:30 next morning and found a room waiting for us at the Grand Hotel. The following morning I discovered a Major of Marines and several naval and marine officers at breakfast and learned that there was a party of seamen and marines stationed there.

"They expected to be withdrawn by sea that night, but no ship came. During the whole of daylight hours there was a continual succession of air-raid alarms. A few bombs were dropped, but, on the whole, the town was very little damaged. The following day Smith and I decided to push on to Aandalsnes. We set out at noon in a car provided by the Norwegian authorities, and each with a borrowed revolver and ammunition.

"We had an eventful journey, having to jump out

of the car and hide in the woods and ditches on numerous occasions to avoid being machine-gunned and bombed, but managed to drive through what remained of the town safely and reported to force headquarters, where we were given a very welcome meal, not having eaten since breakfast. Bombing continued until 10 P.M., and at 11 we joined in the final evacuation of the town."

The lives lost in the fiasco at Namsos were not thrown away, since the Allied failure brought to a head the slowly gathering awareness of the British democracy and of its representatives in Parliament that the direction of the war was in feeble hands and that the situation was critical in the extreme.

After the fiasco of Norway Chamberlain at last was driven to resign, and in the most desperate hour of British history Winston Churchill formed a new government. All responsible men knew that Britain would be told the truth and, knowing it, would at last be able to use her strength. And with the first of Churchill's broadcasts fear left us: he told us he brought us nothing but blood, sweat, and tears. Many of us knew it already, and in the midst of our disasters we were happy, for we had faith in our own people, and our hearts were right.

The Allied withdrawal from Namsos and the destruction of the Gladiator squadron at Aandalsnes was not the end of the Norwegian campaign. There was the postscript of Narvik, the tragic story of which was overshadowed by that of France. Since it has hardly been told, I shall describe the part played by the Royal Air Force in some detail.

Narvik, as I have said, was the port from which iron ore from the Swedish mines across the frontier was shipped, particularly during the winter months when Lulea in the Baltic is icebound.

Protection for our land and sea forces operating against Narvik and occupying the town after its capture was provided by two fighter squadrons, one of Gladiators and the other of Hurricanes.

An advance party had been sent to prepare landing grounds. There was perpetual daylight, and the country, when they arrived, was still under snow. On the one side there were the winding inlets of the fjords among the islands; on the other valleys deep in snow led up to the high mountains on the Swedish frontier, often lost in cloud.

Three sites were chosen but, as two of them were never really serviceable, they can be ignored, though the men working desperately upon them and exposed to the bombs and machine guns of the enemy should be remembered.

Bardu was under three feet of snow below which there was a foot of ice. Shifts of a thousand Norwegians were kept working continuously twenty-four hours a day. Two runways were made. When the snow had been cleared there was a thaw. When the ice below had been all blasted and removed it melted everywhere, and drainage of the torrents of water became necessary. But a sound runway was completed.

On two sides of the landing ground there was thick pine forest. Into this narrow taxiing lanes were cut, and at intervals turnings out of these lanes led to enclosures made of double palisades of tree trunks packed with stones between them. These were covered with wire netting and camouflaged and were invisible, except to a pilot looking down upon them vertically, and then it would be too late for him to bomb.

These enclosures were for the aircraft, to protect them from bombs and splinters. The taxiing lanes and turnings by which the aircraft reached their shelters in the forest were called "the clock-golf course" by our pilots. Besides these other lanes were cut for fire protection.

For the men wigwams were erected, dispersed about the forest where they could eat and sleep. Numerous blastproof shelters were made in convenient places all round the landing ground and the runways, so that all who were not actively engaged in getting an aircraft into the air or serving a gun could take cover when German bombers appeared. Thanks to these precautions, damage to our aircraft on the ground was very slight.

Here is the story of the squadron of Gladiators told in far greater detail than I shall be able to write about other such operations. But there is a tragic unity about the events at Bardu and about its Northern setting of perpetual day.

On May 20 the squadron took off from the aircraft carrier *Glorious*. It was bad weather, and two aircraft of the leading section crashed into a mountainside, and their pilots were killed. The other aircraft returned to the *Glorious* safely, though, not being members of the Fleet Air Arm, none of them had made deck landings before.

On May 21 they all reached Bardu safely by 9 A.M.

The task of the squadron was to give air protection to our military base and to our shipping, to patrol an area of about ten square miles, and keep hostile aircraft out of it. Later a standing patrol over the town of Narvik was maintained.

On the twenty-second fifty-four sorties were made against the enemy. One pilot who failed to return was found dead in his aircraft on a mountainside close to the wreckage of a He. 111.

On the twenty-third forty sorties were carried out.

One He. 111 is believed to have been shot down by a sergeant who had to bale out. This reduced the squadron to fourteen aircraft.

On the twenty-fourth, during the afternoon, two Gladiators attacked a Heinkel and put the rear gunner and one engine out of action. A third pilot, returning from patrol, joined in and put the He. 111's other engine out of action, and it crashed.

On May 25 forty sorties were carried out.

At 9 A.M. a pilot attacked a Ju. 90 four-engined heavy bomber which forced-landed. At ten-thirty the same pilot attacked another Ju. 90 out of the sun, shot the rear gunner with his first burst, and then with four successive short bursts disabled each of the four engines in turn. The Ju. 90 crashed in flames.

At 8:30 P.M. two pilots attacked a third Ju. 90 which was bombing a destroyer. They put the rear gunner and one engine out of action, after which it crashed into the sea.

Next day, May 26, the squadron carried out over fifty sorties. At ten-thirty two pilots attacked a Ju. 88, disabling one engine. Part of the wing fell off, and it went down in flames.

At one o'clock three pilots flew to Bodo aerodrome, where all three aircraft became bogged. As soon as they were dug out two He. 111s appeared. Two of the Gladiators took off and chased them away. On landing, one of the Gladiators crashed in the soft ground. More hostile aircraft appeared. One of the Gladiators took off again and attacked an He. 111, which made off, with smoke pouring from its engines. The pilot then attacked a Ju. 52, which crashed in flames. Two more Ju. 52s appeared. Our pilot attacked the second which spun into the ground. He next attacked a Heinkel 111, damaged both its engines, and shot the rear gunner, after which he landed, with his own guns out of action.

While this was going on at Bodo the pilots at Bardu were also busy. At 1 P.M two of them attacked a Do. 17, which crashed in the hills. One of our pilots broke off this combat to attack five other Do. 17s flying in formation. He attacked number three, which crashed. The remainder escaped.

At 3 P.M. two other pilots on patrol attacked five He. 111s. One pilot made an attack on number two. The He. crashed, but our pilot was wounded in the neck and chest. The other pilot attacked number four of the formation, which crashed.

On May 27 an air-raid alarm was given, and about a dozen Ju. 87s and Me. 110s began dive bombing the jetty. The two pilots with serviceable aircraft at Bodo took off. The pilot who had done so well there the day before attacked a Ju. 87 which is known to have sunk later in the sea. Shortly afterwards he was hit in the head and knee by the rear gunner of another Ju. 87. The Gladiator fell out of control with locked ailerons, but the wounded pilot regained control at a height of two hundred feet and succeeded in making a crash landing in the hills. He was taken to hospital and later awarded the D.F.C. The other pilot found himself ringed in by hostile aircraft and unable to land. He received several bullet wounds, and though he made a crash landing his aircraft was destroyed. This brought the numbers of the squadron down to eleven aircraft.

On May 27 at Bardu a sergeant attacked three He. 111s but was himself attacked by another He. 111 which he had not seen. He made four attacks on it, and it crashed in a valley.

At six o'clock the same sergeant attacked another He. 111, which escaped.

On May 28 at seven-thirty one of the pilots on patrol attacked an He. 111 which was dive-bombing a cruiser. He set it on fire, and it is regarded as certain that it crashed.

On May 29 at 11 A.M. three He. 111s attacked Bardu Foss. The sergeant previously mentioned chased them and attacked one over Narvik and fired two bursts into it. It crashed.

On May 30, 31, and June 1 the weather was bad, and no enemy aircraft came over. During this time twenty-two ground-strafing raids were carried out by the

Gladiator squadron on German troops and trains of lorries, much execution being done against the latter. One Gladiator received some damage from fire from the ground.

On June 2 there were fifty-five sorties by the squadron, besides the continuous standing patrol over Narvik.

At 1 P.M. two pilots met twelve to fifteen hostile aircraft at fourteen thousand feet. They made a simultaneous attack on the rear aircraft of a formation of four He. 111s, which crashed in flames. They next attacked number three, which crashed. They then made seven attacks on the remaining two of the formation, one of which crashed and the other of which escaped. Six Do. 17s were next seen but they jettisoned their bombs and escaped. Later the same pilots met two Ju. 87s, one of which crashed after their attack. One of the pilots then attacked another Ju. 87, which escaped into cloud. His companion attacked an He. 111, which dived beyond the vertical, and he could not follow it. They landed with their ammunition exhausted.

At two-thirty two other pilots on patrol met two Ju. 88s. One of our pilots must have been shot down, for he was not heard of again. The other pilot chased one of the Ju. 88s into Sweden, where he lost it. As he was returning he sighted a Ju. 88 at five hundred feet, which he attacked, and it crashed out of control into the mountainside, wrapped in mist. Coming back he attacked an He. 111, which stalled into the ground. He was then attacked by a Ju. 88 and three He. 111s. He shot down one He. 111 and found himself with two Ju. 88s and six He.s attacking him. His oil tank had been holed by bullets, and his windscreen was covered with oil. He succeeded in shooting down one more He. 111 and then, with ammunition exhausted, managed to make his base.

On the third, fourth, and fifth of June the weather was so bad that there was no flying.

On June 6 there were numerous sorties, but all enemy aircraft jettisoned their bombs and fled at the sight of a British aircraft.

On the seventh of June evacuation of Bardu was completed. At midnight the runway was blown up after the aircraft had flown to H.M. aircraft carrier *Glorious*. Ten Gladiators landed safely on her decks.

And then comes the hideous, hateful sequel. Three hours later the *Glorious* was sunk by the German battle cruisers *Scharnhorst* and *Gneisenau*.

In sixteen days the squadron of Gladiators had lost three aircraft by accidents and five by enemy action. They can be credited with twenty-six confirmed and five unconfirmed victories, all of which were against far more modern and much more expensive aircraft with higher speed. The manoeuvrability and armament of the Gladiator biplane stood it in good stead, but the skill of the pilots and their wonderful fighting spirit was the decisive factor.

A squadron of Hurricanes which was also at Bardu did not do quite so well. They had eleven confirmed and eight unconfirmed victories. Ten of the Hurricane squadron landed safely on the decks of the ill-fated aircraft carrier *Glorious*.

The *Glorious* was avenged by two attacks on the *Scharnhorst*. On June 21 the *Scharnhorst* was located by two of our Sunderland flying boats, and Hudson and Beaufort aircraft were sent to attack her. Three direct hits were scored on the ship, doing much damage and greatly reducing her speed. On the night of the first–second of July the *Scharnhorst* was again attacked as she was undergoing repairs at Kiel. The raiders, Whitley and Hampden heavy bombers, achieved a complete surprise, and there were direct hits and fires on the ship and on both sides of the floating dock. These two ships were, however, eventually repaired and during the winter of 1941 made raids on British shipping, afterwards taking shelter in Brest harbour. Altogether more than forty raids on them were carried out, as a result of which there is reason to hope they have several times sustained severe damage. Many of the raids were carried out at low levels in the face of the most intense anti-aircraft fire.

The raids on these battle cruisers offer a good example of the best use of air power. Ever since they took shelter in Brest they have been immobilized and have played no part in the battle of the Atlantic. They have been ceaselessly under repair—but the repairs are never allowed to be completed. The story of the raids on Brest does not, however, belong here.

CHAPTER IX

The Conquest of Holland

A REMARKABLE FEATURE of the invasion of Norway had been that less than a third of the Luftwaffe had been used in it and that the rest remained at their stations. Thus throughout the Norwegian campaign more than two thirds of the German air force had continued its routine training. The aerodromes far removed from the Western front appeared just as usual while the fate of Norway was being decided. Even though the success of the operations depended upon the rapidity with which troops and their equipment could be flown into the country only three hundred out of a total of more than one thousand troop-carrying aircraft were employed.

The obvious inference was that Germany wished to

strike again in some other theatre at short notice. During the last weeks of April photographic reconnaissances showed that German armoured and mechanized troops were massing on the Belgian and Dutch frontiers and that large numbers of aircraft were being moved to aerodromes in the West.

All these concentrations were allowed to take place without the slightest interference by our bombers, owing to General Gamelin's fear of reprisals. Indeed, I believe that he attempted to maintain his veto for some hours after Germany had violated the Dutch frontiers.

The German air force opened the attack upon Holland at 3:30 A.M. on May 10 by bombing the barracks at The Hague, the Schipol aerodrome near Amsterdam, that of Waalhaven outside Rotterdam, and the three aerodromes of Ypenberg, Ockenburg, and Valkenburg on the outskirts of The Hague. There had been no air-raid alarm, but very thorough preparations had been made in anticipation of an attack. Obstacles such as motorcars were left on the main roads and on aerodromes at night to prevent German aircraft from landing. The object of the German bombing attacks was to destroy aircraft of the Dutch air force on the ground or in hangars without damaging the runways. Many hangars were, in fact, destroyed. After an hour the bombing ceased, and Ju. 52 transport aircraft came over in large numbers with screens of Me. 110 fighters. It was just light. The transport aircraft dropped parachute troops in circles, surrounding the aerodromes, including also those at Delft, Zaandvoord, and the Hook. The parachutists were dropped from a low height, to shorten the time when they would be exposed to fire from the ground, and were dressed in Dutch uniforms. Many of those dropped in Waalhaven were in British uniforms.

The Dutch military authorities actually enquired of the British military and air attachés whether the British were landing troops at Rotterdam. Without wasting time in investigation, they replied that all such parachutists should be shot out of hand.

The use of Dutch uniforms by the parachutists proved very effective. Sentries on guard at the aerodromes did not shoot but stopped to parley and were themselves shot. The parachutists immediately occupied the aerodromes and cleared them of obstructions, so that troop-carrying transports were able to land. The German parachutists failed, however, to capture Ypenberg and were beaten off and shot. The German troop carriers came in and landed there and were greeted with machine-gun fire as they taxied to a standstill. Several of these aircraft were destroyed and the troops in them mown down as they were getting out of the aircraft.

At Waalhaven over a thousand German troops had

been landed before 10 A.M. The aerodrome remained in German hands throughout and became the chief landing ground for German troop carriers.

Later on May 10 Dutch troops succeeded in recapturing the aerodromes at Valkenburg and Ockenburg, with great loss to the Germans. During the morning of May 10 German bombers dropped leaflets on The Hague, calling on the Dutch to surrender, as opposition would be futile. About eleven-thirty bombs were dropped on a maternity hospital in The Hague, killing several patients.

The bombing of Rotterdam was carried out on a huge scale; hundreds, perhaps thousands, of people were killed, and a great part of the city was burned down.

During May 10 several appeals were made by the Dutch for help by the R.A.F. So far as I can learn, the first British aircraft to answer the call were Blenheim fighters from the A.A.S.F. which attacked Waalhaven aerodrome at one-twenty that afternoon, machine-gunning Ju. 52 transports both on the ground and in the air.

The first bombing attack was made on Waalhaven about nine-thirty that night by thirty-six Wellingtons. Next morning the Dutch launched repeated attacks on Waalhaven but failed to recapture it.

More German parachutists were being dropped in the early hours of May 11 at The Hague. Papers carried by one of these men who was captured contained lists

Courtesy of Flight Lieutenant Whitney Straight

GLADIATORS ON A FROZEN CAKE IN NORWAY

of Dutch patriots and of British nationals who were to be rounded up and shot out of hand. There was also the fullest information about all the surroundings, even to the whereabouts of telephone boxes. On the morning of May 11 sniping by Dutch Nazis became general.

German motorized forces had crossed the frontier simultaneously with the air attack. Hundreds of soldiers had also come down the Rhine in barges, without being detected. But a very large number of German troops must have come by air. I believe that, excluding the Lufthansa air liners, there were at this time eight hundred German troop-carrying aircraft capable of transporting twelve thousand men with their equipment at one time. It was simply a matter of holding aerodromes for a few hours and of providing sufficient fighter protection for the Germans to land one or two divisions of troops in this way.

Besides landing troops on the captured aerodromes the less-valuable Lufthansa air liners were used to land troops on the beaches at Scheveningen, Wassenaar, and Katwijk. Numbers of these were damaged on landing, and others were put out of action by machine-gun fire from British aircraft. The story of the extremely well coordinated, well-timed German invasion and of the heroic resistance of the bewildered Dutch who were further embarrassed by large numbers of traitors has yet to be told.

The following combat report by a British pilot officer gives such a vivid picture of the time he spent in Holland and of the state of mind of the Dutch that I print it here in full. A large part of it appeared in *The Times* within a few days of the occurrence.

COMBAT REPORT BY A PILOT OFFICER OF AN ATTACK SOUTH-WEST OF ROTTERDAM, MAY 13, 1940

At 05.45 hours the formation with which I was flying encountered seven Ju. 87s S.W. of Rotterdam. They were not carrying bombs, which might have indicated that they had already bombed their objective. I noticed that Rotterdam was blazing fiercely in several places. The aircraft were immediately formed into line astern and kept turning. I got into position on one Ju. 87, and my air gunner shot down. I saw this aircraft go down, apparently out of control; then afterwards another Ju. 87, which was coming up behind us, was also shot down, apparently out of control. Then about twenty-seven Me. 109s joined in the combat, and I heard my air gunner give a cheer and I think that this meant that he had got an Me. 109 which had been trying to get on my tail. I could not be certain of this, as immediately afterwards the air gunner was killed. I think my starboard tank caught fire, and a stream of bullets came from the rear and shot away the dashboard and part of the control column. I lost control for some time but eventually managed to turn the aircraft on its back, as had been prearranged with the air gunner in order to facilitate baling out. I could get no reply from the air gunner. I baled out when the flames were coming right up the cockpit. I landed on an island southwest of Dordrecht amongst some tall reeds. About one hour later the enemy fighters had disappeared completely. I explored the island, which appeared to be uninhabited, and then went towards a house two miles away in a southeasterly direction. In order to reach this house I had to swim two channels approximately one hundred yards wide. I then saw a house boat moored and climbed on to it. After resting I walked west, keeping the sun behind me, until I came to a house with a barge outside it, but the house was empty. I then found a small boat and rowed for about one hundred yards until I came to a very high dyke. I climbed this and saw another house from which a farm labourer and his wife came to meet me. The time then was approximately 08.00 hours. I managed to make him understand that I was English, as I was carrying my tunic over my arm. By this time the Germans were bombing Dordrecht. This attack lasted all morning. Dordrecht was about fifteen miles away from the farmhouse. This information I got from the farmer. As far as I could see, the aircraft carrying out the bombing were He. 111s and Ju. 87s. At about 12.00 hours the farm labourer locked up the house and rowed me and his family to another island. On the way across I saw twenty Me. 110s which were circling and proceeding further northeast with each circle, which would rather indicate that they were searching the ground for suitable targets to ground-strafe. We eventually reached another farm from which the military were communicated with, and then the labourer offered to take me to the military on the back of his bicycle. After cycling about three miles we came to a dam and were met by Dutch soldiers. It was here that I met P/O H. We were taken in a car to get his arm dressed and after about an hour we were taken to a place called Sleewyk, where we were interrogated by a Dutch intelligence officer who seemed to think I was a German. One of the Dutch officials questioned me and asked where I came from. When I said Swansea I was asked to draw maps of the main streets. We were taken to a hospital, and then a card was tied round my neck on which was written my name, description, and number. My tunic was taken from me here. After being detained for some time in a room with some civilians we were marched to a boat and taken across to Gorinchen, which had apparently been bombed just before we arrived. We were escorted by two guards and were interrogated at police h.q.s by a police officer who could speak good English. We explained that we were British airmen and were asked if we could speak Dutch and were not believed when we said that we could not. I asked the police official to sent a cable to the British Air Ministry and wrote a message out. I do not know whether this message was sent. We were taken then to the military barracks and questioned by an intelligence officer who took all particulars and promised to send a cable to the Air Ministry as well. Two hours later this officer took us by car to The Hague. On the way we ran into a large motorized column of Dutch soldiers. The soldiers searched the car and discovered that our escort was a Fascist. At this point we thought we were going to be shot out of hand. However, eventually we were taken on to The Hague. By this time it was about two in the morning. After a very long time we arrived at The Hague between 5:30 and 6 A.M. We were taken straight to the Dutch military barracks and saw the commanding officer, who spoke perfect English. After we had explained the situation to him we were driven to the British Legation but found everybody had left, so we went to the American Legation, and a Major Colbourne was very helpful indeed. And we finally went in a Buick car, escorted by one soldier and the driver, to the Hook, where there was a British destroyer. During the journey German bombers came over, and five Blenheims were also seen. Eventually a British naval officer allowed us to board the destroyer, and we landed at Dover at 7:30 P.M. on the fourteenth of May, 1940.

The Dutch air force numbered some 250 aircraft. By the morning of May 13 only ten of these aircraft were still in existence; by the evening these last ten had been destroyed. During the first day's fighting the Dutch fighters and anti-aircraft are believed to have shot down 154 German aircraft. Only two of the Dutch fleet of K.L.M. air liners escaped to Britain. The rest were captured by the Germans or destroyed.

The Queen of Holland and the Dutch government left Holland on the evening of May 13 for England.

Soon afterwards the Dutch commander in chief, realizing the absolutely hopeless situation of the troops under his command, surrendered to the Germans.

The conception of German operations in the West—in Norway as well as Holland, Belgium, and France—was apparently that of General Jerschonnek, who received the Knight's Cross of the Iron Cross for the planning and execution of the air operations against Poland.

He was promoted full general in July 1940. General Jerschonnek is believed to have the most able and original mind in the German air force. He must be credited in particular with the very close cooperation of aircraft and tanks and motorized troops. He has been Chief of Air Staff since February 1939. Jerschonnek joined the German army at the age of sixteen in 1915 and was shortly afterwards transferred to the flying corps. He was a fighter pilot until the end of the war. He is now only forty years old and is perhaps the most formidable opponent Britain has today.

CHAPTER X

The Invasion of France

ALMOST SIMULTANEOUSLY with the invasion of Holland, German mechanized columns crossed the frontiers of Luxemburg and Belgium and French and British troops entered Belgium shortly afterwards, a move which was to prove disastrous. German parachutists in Belgian uniform are reported to have prevented the blowing up of bridges over the Meuse and to have been instrumental in the capture of the fort of Eben-emael.

The failure of the Belgians to destroy the bridges and later to hold Maastricht proved disastrous, for the French army holding the line of the Meuse below Namur found itself in an untenable position.

Two main German attacks developed. The columns which had advanced through Luxemburg broke through the French defences at Sedan. Further north the armoured divisions which had crossed the Meuse attacked the French "ninth army" which was attempting to hold the line from Wavre, through Gembloux, to Namur. Gembloux was the centre of this northern attack.

The British expeditionary force holding the line of the river Dyle to the east of Brussels was not heavily attacked at this time and throughout all the operations until its final evacuation showed itself to be the master of the enemy. The British troops who actually fought with the Germans were puzzled and angry at the retreat.

Air operations on the German side were almost entirely devoted to two objects: to cooperation with the ground forces in smashing centres of allied resistance by dive-bombing attacks and to maintaining the necessary ascendancy in the air by intercepting allied aircraft and by attacks on allied aerodromes.

It is true there was a spectacular daylight bombing raid on Paris and that the operations had been preceded by bombing raids on the Rhone valley. But these raids were of minor importance, and the main weight of the German air force was devoted to tactical cooperation with the German armoured divisions. Against the Dutch, Belgians, British, and French the Germans threw the entire first-line strength of their air force, excluding only those engaged in Norway.

As during the campaign in Poland, every motorized column of troops and tanks and of the infantry which struggled slowly after them was able to call up help from army-cooperation and dive-bombing aircraft which were available when needed, and at short notice, and also had its own "Flak" detachment of anti-aircraft guns and machine guns.

It should be noted that units of the German ground forces do not have definite numbers of aircraft allotted to them or under their command. They call up aircraft as required, and the rapidity with which air cooperation was always available shows that the staff work of the German air force was beyond praise.

The operations very closely resembled those in Poland, but there was even more perfect cooperation between mechanized ground forces and the dive bombers which were relied upon to blast a way through when really serious opposition was met with.

It is worth considering the reasons for the success of the German dive bomber. It is not enough to attribute the rout of the French army to German tanks and dive bombers. The Germans owed victory as much to lack of equipment in the Allied armies as to the excellence of their own. It has been stated on good authority that the German army was provided with anti-aircraft defences on a scale at least ten times as great as that of the British and French. It follows from this that had the Allies possessed dive bombers they could not have achieved anything like the same result with them as the

Germans. Even as it was, the German losses of dive bombers were heavy. Owing to the overwhelming German numbers, they could be accepted.

The German success is therefore unlikely to be repeated by the British at any time in the future. It depended upon so many factors: upon command of the air due to weakness of the French and British in fighters, upon their lack of anti-aircraft, upon the moral effect of a new and terrifyingly noisy weapon. The moral effect of the dive bomber, all observers are agreed, was far greater than the material results. It was due to lack of anti-aircraft defences.

The strength of the German anti-aircraft made British and French defensive bombing extremely expensive and greatly reduced the scale of our daylight bombing defences. The German superiority in daylight bombers was not only in numbers. It was much more than that. For the probable life of each German bomber far exceeded the probable life of the bombers we sent to delay their advance. Thus each German bomber was (apart from anything else) that much more efficient. It is hardly necessary to point out that the bomber which has been shot down cannot be sent out again on another raid.

Finally the German victory was largely due to the spell of dry and perfect weather which lasted from the beginning of the attack until its conclusion. A week of rainy or foggy days in the middle of May might easily have saved France. Even as it was, the operations in France were far more of a gamble than those in Poland, which could not very well have failed, for, having broken through at Sedan and Gembloux and having utterly routed the army of General Corap, the Panzerdivisionen went straight across France. By the eighteenth of May German tanks were approaching Peronne, and in the next few days several armoured divisions had passed through the gap between Cambrai and Peronne and were racing for the channel ports. They were ten days or a fortnight ahead of the German infantry.

If General Weygand's plan of a simultaneous attack north from the Somme and south from Douai and Arras had been carried out the German spearhead would have been cut off and would have been in the greatest peril. The entire position would have been reversed. Such a plan depended for its execution upon a reserve of stiff troops. Two British divisions attacked from the north on May 21, but the French corps on the left failed to cooperate, and the attack from the Somme failed to materialize. A further attempt was to have been made by the British and a French corps to close the gap by an attack from the north on May 26, but by that time the Belgian front had collapsed, and a rapid retreat to Dunkirk was imperative if the British were not to be cut off from the sea. They had already been cut off from their bases.

No complete picture can be given of the German air operations in the conquest of the Low Countries and of France. At present all that can be done is to give partial and fragmentary indications of them from the point of view of the Royal Air Force. Besides the greater use of the dive bomber, the following points, however, do emerge: Attacks on aerodromes, outside Holland, were less successful than in Poland. The dispersion of aircraft and anti-aircraft defences made low-flying attacks un-profitable. A German low-flying attack on a British aerodrome in France, defended with only sixteen Lewis guns, cost the enemy eight aircraft, while only six British fighters were destroyed on the ground. I believe that the French losses from attacks on aerodromes were higher than those of the British.

Deliberate attacks were made on masses of refugees moving on the roads even when there were no troops near by or mixed up with them.

The scale of these operations involving the entire populations of Holland, Belgium, and northern France can scarcely be realized. Millions of men armed with the most deadly weapons of war were moving forward, fighting, killing, stubbornly retreating, or frankly running away. Thousands of tanks rattled along the roads, deployed over the fields, sought shelter in woods, broke through the walls of orchards into old-world Flemish gardens. One must visualize the unexpectedness of the attack. Holland and Belgium had been at peace one day. Let us imagine one garden where gardeners were planting out vegetables or admiring the rows of tulips. Two days later the tank tracks had smashed all into the earth, and a party of Belgian cyclists or a postman had been cut off and surprised with death beyond the breaches in the garden wall. And one must multiply such images a thousand and a thousand times again before one can begin to understand what we are speaking of.

One must remember, too, that it was early summer, the weather warm and dry, the days long and the most beautiful of the year. Dawn came, and in the fields and forests the birds took up their task of feeding their nestlings, caring little for the tired men who had snatched a few hours of sprawling sleep out of doors.

Often in the darkness the sleepers had sat up and clutched their rifles as the roar of bombers swept overhead and then had watched the spouts of flame flung up and felt the earth shudder as the bombs exploded. When they rose to march they found the roads and byways choked with the black crowd of refugees. Strangely laden automobiles hooted senselessly at the people on foot who hemmed them in and would not move out of the way. They were like the crowds hurry-

ing to a race meeting, except that there were few young
men and so many of the very old and of the very young.
And suddenly the crowd would halt in terror, gazing
upwards at the black crosses on the wings, and surge
this way and that towards the ditches on either side as
the bullets spattered, leaving dead, wounded, and dying
—children, old men, women—upon the road. And in a
few minutes the pools of blood where the bodies had
lain would be caking dust upon the boots of those
pressing onwards to escape somehow from the
Boches.

The battle in the air was on a proportionate scale to
that on land but less senseless, more intelligent, more
heroic.

The immense value of unity of command given by an
independent air force was shown. All branches of the
Royal Air Force were thrown in to delay the enemy,
according to a coordinated plan.

From the first day Bomber Command put into operation its plans of the strategic offensive, bombing German railways, marshalling yards, synthetic-oil plants,
and refineries. Attacks were made on the Dutch aerodromes and on focal points in the German advance.
Thus at 9 P.M. on May 10, the day on which the Germans had captured Waalhaven aerodrome, thirty-six
of our Wellingtons launched an attack upon it, after
which German aircraft had to land in neighbouring

fields. The Royal Air Force made a second attack upon Waalhaven during the night of May 12.

From the time of the German crossing of the Meuse the main effort of Bomber Command was expended in France and Belgium chiefly in night raids on German rear communications. Nothing is more striking at this period than the contrast of our losses in day and night bombing.

On May 17 twelve Blenheims were sent to attack Gembloux by day. Only one returned. Forty-six Wellingtons and five Hampdens took up the attack by night, and all returned safely. Again on May 19 thirty Wellingtons attacked Gembloux by night, and all returned. On the night of the twentieth seventy-three heavy bombers and eighteen Blenheims attacked enemy rear communications. Four failed to return. On the night of the twenty-first seventeen Wellingtons attacked the Meuse crossings, Liége and Maastricht, and three failed to return. On the night of the twenty-third forty-eight Wellingtons attacked Gembloux, Charleroi, and the Meuse crossings, and all returned. Such losses in the circumstances are astonishingly light. In considering whether day bombing is worth while it is necessary to be able to sum up the probabilities involved and to remember that the bomber which has a probable life of two days if sent against a particularly strongly defended target by day will have a probable life of two months or more if sent to bomb it at night. And the greater accuracy of day bombing is not proportionate to the greater risk attending it.

While these operations were being carried out by the heavy bombers Coastal Command aircraft attacked the oil-storage tanks at Rotterdam and enemy motor torpedo boats off the Dutch and Belgian coasts. In the week ending the fifth of June there were thirty-six attacks by Coastal Command aircraft against oil refineries. Covering patrols off the Belgian coast were also provided throughout the evacuation of Dunkirk, during which enemy motor torpedo boats were repeatedly attacked.

The air component of fighters and army-cooperation aircraft worked with the B.E.F. until the end. Before the Germans reached the aerodromes in France the air component was evacuated but continued taking an active part in the battle from bases in Kent. Thirty-eight Lysanders were used to drop food for the defenders of Calais.

In the earlier stages of the battle, during the advance into Belgium, Fighter Command aircraft based on aerodromes in southeast England flew daily to France to refuelling points from which they operated throughout the day, giving fighter cover to the left flank of the Allied armies. Unfortunately the French aerodromes were unsuitable and were frequently attacked by the enemy, so that after May 20 it was found more efficient for our fighters to operate from refuelling points on the Kent coast. During the withdrawal of the B.E.F., protection from German dive bombers was more urgently needed, and more fighters were employed for this purpose. The fighter cover provided for the evacuation of troops from Dunkirk will be discussed in the next chapter.

On May 10 several of the A.A.S.F. aerodromes were bombed by enemy aircraft. Blenheims were sent to bomb the aerodromes which the enemy had seized in Holland, and squadrons of Battles were sent to bomb the German troops advancing through Luxemburg. Both Blenheims and Battles were employed in the earlier phases of the battle of France to make low-flying attacks by day against the advancing enemy. These served to delay his advance, but our aircraft suffered very severe losses. In the later stages of the battle our losses from such ground-strafing were not nearly so great. This seems to have been because in the early stages the Germans were working to an exact plan by which every column was given the fullest possible anti-aircraft protection as it advanced. As the battle developed and the front became widely extended this could not be done on the same scale, and their anti-aircraft protection became dispersed.

Since the French and Belgians failed to blow up

bridges over the Meuse and other rivers and canals, the R.A.F. was called upon to bomb many bridges. The bombing of bridges from the air is an exceedingly difficult operation. Nothing but a direct hit is of any use, and our losses in bombing bridges were extremely heavy.

On May 14 sixty-seven bombers were sent to attack bridges near Sedan, and thirty-five failed to return. The story of how volunteers were called for to blow up two bridges over the Albert Canal from the pilots of a squadron of Fairey Battles has often been told. All volunteered. Names were then put in a hat and the required number drawn. Of the five crews sent only two men returned alive. In contrast to these terrible operations by day we find on the night of May 18–19 twelve Wellingtons and eleven Hampdens attacked the crossings of the Meuse, and all returned safely.

The bombing of bridges which the French had failed to blow up or of German pontoons continued necessary by day, but our losses greatly decreased. Between June 5 and June 14 of seventy-eight sorties to bomb bridges only three aircraft failed to return. This was undoubtedly also because German anti-aircraft protection became less effective as the area they occupied became greater.

It was also partly due to our employing Blenheims rather than Battles in these daylight operations. Owing

to their vulnerability to German fighter attack, our
Battle squadrons in the later stages were used for night
operations only. No doubt this possibility has been fore-
seen, and the insistence on their being given training in
night flying proved a wise precaution.

The Battle squadrons were used at night to bomb
German motorized units and tanks resting in woods, to
bomb ammunition dumps and congested centres of communication. In all these night-flying operations the
crews showed astonishing endurance, putting in more
hours' flying than it had been thought possible to ask of
any aircraft crews under any conditions.

The fact that there were a certain number of surplus
crews for our Blenheims enabled these to be used for
both day and night operations. The heavy bombers of
Bomber Command, which were not part of the
A.A.S.F., were only used at night during the battle of
France. Their task was to hold up the German armies
by delaying their supplies far behind the front. For this
purpose they attacked German railway marshalling
yards and bombed bottlenecks on the roads where German supply columns were congested. Their work would
have been far more effective if the French civil population had been trained what to do in the event of a German advance. As it was, the population made military
movements on the roads extremely slow and difficult,
and they left all their possessions for the Germans, who

were able to live on the country, obtaining their food and finding supplies of fuel in the petrol pumps. If the civil population had been taught to destroy everything likely to be of use to the advancing Germans France might have never been conquered.

The French requests for more British fighters to be sent to France proved amply justified. A far greater number than those in the Hurricane squadrons of the B.A.A.F. was needed. In the first place, had we had more fighters in France the losses of our bombers would not have been so heavy. In the second, much larger numbers of enemy aircraft would have been destroyed. As it was, three fighter squadrons in the A.A.S.F. shot down one hundred and fifty enemy aircraft for certain and twenty-five probables between May 10 and June 6. But it was to support the morale of the French troops under German dive-bombing attacks that more of our fighters were so desperately needed. The lesson of Poland had not been learned, chiefly because both the French and British High Commands had believed in the overwhelming strength of prepared positions and had underrated the Polish army. Had we had more fighters in France the outcome of the battle for France might have been different. It was the German dive bombers which made the break-through possible. Again and again the German tanks would have been held up had they not been able to "whistle up their air."

Yet, having made the mistake of not sending enough fighters to France, the Air Ministry showed the highest wisdom in not sending and in refusing to send them to French bases at the last moment. Fighters are short-range aircraft and they have to return to their bases at short intervals for refuelling and rearming. They continually received damage in air combats which has to be immediately repaired. Quite apart from the absolute necessity of maintaining the defences of Britain intact, if large numbers of fighter squadrons had been sent to France at the last moment they would have been wasted. That is to say, they could only have achieved a fraction of what they did a few weeks later, operating from their own well-equipped bases. Aircraft inadequately maintained are wasted, and once the battle of France had begun it was impossible to transport all the ground personnel, fitters, riggers, mechanics, with their benches, workshops, tools, and stores of spare parts, and get them immediately into full working order. The aerodromes for their reception did not exist. And then it would have been impossible to bring them home again had they failed to stay the German advance.

It is a first rule in warfare to concentrate one's forces at the decisive point. We could not have saved France by answering her last-minute appeal, by dividing our forces. The Air Ministry, as events have proved, were justified a thousand times over, on technical grounds alone, in refusing the appeals for fighters once the battle of France had been joined. In point of fact, the number of fighters with the air component of the B.E.F. was increased on May 12, and fighter cover was given on the Western flank, during the advance into Belgium, and the retreat by fighters based on Britain.

The rapidity of the German advance soon threatened the advanced aerodromes of the A.A.S.F., and directly withdrawal became necessary the effectiveness of the B.A.F.F. was inevitably decreased. Such evacuation was not undertaken until it was absolutely necessary. Thus on the fifteenth and sixteenth of May the Germans reached Rethel, within ten miles of an A.A.S.F. aerodrome in full operation. Immediate withdrawal was ordered and, as the French had not allocated aerodromes in the rear for the A.A.S.F., it had to be made to our own aerodromes which were under construction on sites acquired by the British Air Ministry. Owing to this withdrawal, many of our bombers were out of action for two days.

On May 29 the A.A.S.F. withdrew to Vendome, maintaining advanced landing grounds in the neighbourhood of Troyes, from which they continued operations until the twelfth of June, when the German advance reached the latter.

On June 15 plans for evacuation were completed.

The squadrons of the A.A.S.F. after a final sortie were ordered to refuel and to fly to Britain. Embarkation of the ground staff was successfully completed on June 17, the day on which the French asked for an armistice. Three squadrons of fighters remained till the last moment to give protection to all ships. They were unfortunately unable to protect the liner *Lancastria*, which was sunk, with about five thousand airmen and troops on board, soon after she left port. A large number of lives was lost. The enemy aircraft came down and machine-gunned our men swimming in the water.

The evacuation of the A.A.S.F. was otherwise an extremely fine piece of work. All aircraft fit to fly were flown to Britain; all unserviceable aircraft were burned. All spare engines and practically all technical stores were evacuated, though large quantities of fuel and ammunition were undoubtedly abandoned in moving from one base to another.

During the battle of France a heavy bomber base was established in record time at Marseilles for use against Italy. As events turned out, it was not of much use, though Genoa was bombed twice. Unfortunately bad weather prevented most of our aircraft from reaching their objectives. On one occasion a raid on Italy was prevented by the French who drove lorries onto the aerodrome.

On the seventeenth of June evacuation was ordered, but, owing to the lack of facilities for loading the ships, some stores has to be left at Toulon.

Unfortunately I have little knowledge of the part played by the French air force in the battle of France. Thus what should be a separate chapter is reduced to a mere postscript. As has been said already, the French suffered severe losses, and their efficiency was reduced because, although their air force was weak, their aerodromes were congested.

After the armistice about six hundred aircraft of various types of those which remained to the French air force were flown, or otherwise evacuated, to North Africa, together with numbers of pilots and personnel of the ground staff.

Other French pilots, disgusted at the terms of the armistice and the character of the Vichy government, escaped to Britain and are now serving with the Free French forces.

As the war goes on it seems certain that Britain will receive more and more help from the French.

It was in no way the fault of the French air force that a most cruel blow was struck at Britain and at the Royal Air Force by our French allies. This was the liberation of over four hundred German pilots and airmen captured during the fighting in France, many of them by the gallantry of British fighter pilots. During the critical days the British government asked several times that these men should be handed over to us and sent to Britain for safekeeping. Germany was much shorter of pilots than of aircraft at this period, and the surrender of these men must have resulted in the loss of many hundred British lives during the months which followed. For example, I have seen it stated that members of the crew of an He. 111 which made a forced landing in Kent on September 11 were among these men. They had been taken prisoner just before the armistice, released five days later, and after they had successfully bombed the Docks their aircraft was hit by A.A. fire, and they were made prisoners again. This time it was for the duration of the war.

The surrender of these men was the act which we found it hardest to forgive our ally in her extremity. It must always be remembered, however, that it was the act of a small number of men who had already brought their own country to ruin. France's sufferings and defeat have made her more beloved and Nazi Germany more hated by British people than when we set out together to defend the liberties of Europe.

I have even less information about the Belgian air force, which was weak in numbers and in quality. It consisted chiefly of obsolete types of British aircraft, such as Fairey Foxes and Fireflies.

CHAPTER XI

The Battle over Dunkirk

IN THREE WEEKS German arms and military genius had defeated the armies of four countries. The Dutch army split up, surprised and overwhelmed from the air, had surrendered with honour when its position had been rendered hopeless. The King of the Belgians had surrendered. The French armies had been broken in pieces, and the remnants were being driven to the Loire. The B.E.F., with its northern flank suddenly exposed after King Leopold had surrendered, had only saved itself from annihilation by the most rapid of retreats. The King appears to have informed the British and French governments before surrendering, but the news apparently did not reach British headquarters.

Driven back onto the coast it seemed that without too much difficulty some two hundred and twenty thousand British troops could be exterminated or bombed into surrender within hearing and almost within sight of Kent. Nothing, it seemed, could save the most hated, because the most dangerous, of Hitler's enemies. Footsore and exhausted by desperate forced marches and stubborn rear-guard actions, the British had retreated until they could go no further and were crowding, in their tens of thousands, upon an open beach.

Like the Kaiser before him, Hitler might well have regarded the British army as contemptible, and, though that view might not have been shared by those German soldiers who had been foremost in pursuit, all alike would have agreed that it was doomed. In the retreat the British had abandoned their artillery, their stores, and most of their heavier equipment. Thousands of soldiers had only succeeded in reaching the coast by throwing away their packs and their rifles and were without any means of continuing to fight.

German dive bombers had shown what they could do in the destruction of the Basque town of Guernica and since the trials of their quality in Spain they had cut the Polish army into pieces, had nullified British help to Norway, had sent the army of General Corap flying in wild panic from the Meuse. They had bombed into silence, one after another, all the strong points where the French soldiers fought resolutely against the German tanks. The price of recent victories had been high, but here at least they would reap their reward. They would kill and kill and kill. Easy meat was stretched below along the Channel coast. To slaughter the British in tens of thousands would seem to Germans to be humane, and Goering, who had created the German air force for this very purpose, had assured a public audience that he was humane. With the flower of her army gone, Britain would be forced to realize that further resistance was useless and would surrender at discretion.

The British navy would, in that event, fall into German hands and become available for further conquests. The British Empire would be cut up. Under the direction of professional traitors like Lord Haw-Haw, assisted by experts of the Nazi S.S., British life would be purified of its Liberals, its Socialists, its Capitalists, its intellectuals, its Trade Union leaders, its scientists, its artists, and its Jews. The remainder of the British people, under the leadership of British Fascists, would learn what cooperation with Germany would mean.

All this would follow when the bombers of the German air force had done their work. And on the beaches of Dunkirk the British army was in poor shape to defend itself.

The destruction of the British army ought not to have been a difficult matter. Interference must, of course, be expected from the fighters of the Royal Air Force, but there were plenty of German fighters to escort and protect their bombers. There would also, no doubt, be heavy anti-aircraft fire, chiefly from British ships and destroyers, but these must be engaged by other bombers and attacked by the high-speed German motor torpedo boats which, using Dutch and Belgian bases, were waiting to attack any ships which succeeded in taking troops off from Dunkirk.

The bombers and fighters of the Luftwaffe were already using as their advanced bases the aerodromes they had captured in Holland and northern France and those which King Leopold had handed over to them.

They had only to ferry their bombs down a short stretch of coast or for a few minutes across the plain of Flanders and to drop them where the crowds were packed thickest on the beach.

Such was the task before the Luftwaffe. Yet the German bombers failed. The British expeditionary force was brought home to Britain, without its arms, its equipment, or its stores. Yet 186,587 British troops were brought off the beaches of Dunkirk to fight another day, and less than thirty thousand of the B.E.F. were left prisoners in France, a figure which includes all the stragglers and wounded men who were unable during the retreat to reach the coast. Moreover, 123,095 French troops were also evacuated. Why did the Luftwaffe fail? The first answer, and the most important, is that the British navy commanded the Channel. The second is that the British are a seagoing people, and every available seaman helped. And the third reason is that the sailors were able to do their job, thanks to Fighter Command.

Early in the proceedings the Germans had bombed the jetty at Dunkirk and had set on fire the oil-storage tanks there. Both these achievements made their task more difficult. Owing to the destruction of the jetty, troop transports could not come into the harbour and load up there. Instead of that the troops had to be taken in small boats off the miles of beach to the ships which would take them across the channel. Thus, instead of a small number of large and easy targets, the bombers of the Luftwaffe were presented with a very large number of small and difficult ones. Moreover, the pall of black smoke from the burning oil tanks hung like a cloud across the seashore, following the coast line. Many of our fighters, when hardest pressed by superior numbers and with their ammunition expended, found safety by diving into this pall of smoke where it was thickest.

With remarkable foresight the British Admiralty, some little while before the evacuation became necessary, had asked the owners of small craft—motor launches and yachts—to loan them to the government and to volunteer to man them if possible. Many hundreds had responded. As everybody knows, these small vessels were then mobilized. Dozens of them came down the Thames, where they had been laid up since the declaration of war. More of them came from yachting centres round the coasts—from Cowes, Harwich, Yarmouth, and the Norfolk Broads.

The mobilization and sailing of these yachts was an amazing piece of impromptu. But they got to Dunkirk, and the majority managed to get a certain number of soldiers off the beach. The weather for the first days of the evacuation was extremely rough. The sea is shallow, and the coast is sandy and in rough weather can only be approached at high tide. An extraordinary collection of vessels of all kinds, from "mudhoppers," which carry the dredged mud from the Thames estuary out to dump it in deep water, to famous racing cutters, lay either anchored or moved about offshore. They were within sight of the crowds of troops but unable, owing to the combination of low tide and high seas, to rescue any.

The collection of the small craft and getting them across the Channel had been a good idea, but some of them proved useless during the very rough weather of the first days. Clinker-built racing boats are not constructed to take a pounding on the bottom. They were dependent on their auxiliary motors, and many of them lost propeller blades, strained seams, were pooped in breakers, and thrown up, wrecked, upon the beach. Masefield tells us that soldiers' overcoats, discarded in the water, were continually fouling propellers.

Meanwhile, however, some clearheaded fellow had sent orders for all the lifeboats on the south and east coasts of Britain to be sent to Dunkirk. Built for launching and landing in the roughest seas, with ample carrying capacity, very powerful engines, and highly trained crews, the lifeboats were ideal for the work.

The evacuation of the B.E.F. lasted from May 29 until the night of the second–third of June. Evacuation of the French army was completed by June 5. During that time 186,587 British troops, 6,981 wounded, and 123,095 of the French had been brought safely to Britain. Less than thirty thousand British troops, including all those who had fallen out on the retreat, who had been wounded, and who had been cut off, were taken prisoner.

The Luftwaffe had been powerless to affect the issue seriously, thanks to the pilots of Fighter Command.

At Dunkirk British fighters were fighting under great handicaps. All the tactical advantages were enjoyed by the German air force. Owing to their heavy armament, our Spitfires and Hurricanes are short-range aircraft and they were at this time operating at the extreme limits of their range. To refuel and rearm they had to return across the sea. That means that if any pilot miscalculated the fuel remaining in his tanks and went on fighting or patrolling a little too long he was going to come down in the sea. A German fighter in the same cir-

DUNKIRK FROM THE SHORE

A remarkable panoramic view of the two oil tanks burning furiously. The aircraft in the right foreground is a Coastal Command *Lockheed Hudson* on patrol. The picture gives an excellent impression of the shallow beach from which the B.E.F. had to be embarked.

cumstances could come down in some French or Belgian field.

Nearly every British pilot who had to bale out was either taken prisoner or came down in the sea. Not all such pilots were picked up. We lost numbers of aircraft, owing to these causes—aircraft we could very ill spare. And we lost many pilots who were far more precious to us than aircraft. Here is the combat report of one who was picked up.

REPORT BY A FLIGHT SERGEANT OF A PATROL OVER DUNKIRK ON MAY 28, 1940

I was "X" in a formation of nine aircraft patrolling Dunkirk. Towards the end of our patrol about 9 Me. 109s were sighted. A dogfight ensued, and a Me. 109 sailed in front of me and started climbing away from me. I opened fire at one hundred yards, and the second burst set him on fire. I then turned right, onto another Me. 109, and fired one burst from astern; his port wing folded up. As I levelled out a Ju. 88 flew across my path. I did a quarter attack on him. His starboard engine emitted black smoke, and he half rolled into the sea.

I was then hit underneath by a cannon shell and did a complete turn to the right and saw an Me. 110 flying past. I did a beam attack on him, and his starboard engine smoked, and he turned on his back and fell in the sea. I then turned to the right and saw a large number of enemy aircraft, so I turned sharply to the left and saw at least eighty enemy aircraft proceeding for the direction of Dover. A number of them immediately turned onto me, and I pulled the plug and headed for home, twisting and turning.

Whichever way I turned I ran into incendiary fire, and the aircraft was hit a number of times. Two shells smashed the instrument panel, and three more struck underneath. The engine stopped, and flames appeared over the wing roots. I was at four hundred feet and tried to get out but couldn't, so I pulled the stick back for a crouching position on the seat. As the aircraft stalled, I got over the port side and took a header off the main plane.

I was being fired at, so I delayed pulling the rip cord until I was about two hundred feet above the sea. I left the aircraft at eight hundred feet. The parachute worked perfectly; my lifesaving jacket held me up well with one deep breath in it. I was picked up by the paddle steamer *Sundown* and landed at Margate.

A pilot's troubles are by no means over when he has baled out and his parachute has opened. If he has no friends at hand to protect him he becomes an easy target for German aircraft. Sometimes his friends may be as dangerous as enemies or, at all events, as hostile in intention.

Another combat report by a pilot officer of a flight over Dunkirk on May 27 runs as follows:

We engaged the enemy over the sea about a mile from Dunkirk. I attacked the enemy for a few seconds but found another Hurricane attacking as well and, as he was better placed than myself, I turned away to look for something new. I was flying towards Dunkirk when out of the oil smoke which lies thick over the town and dead ahead of me approached a Me. 110. We had no time for anything but a head-on attack, and, for the brief space I had him in my sights, I must have damaged him severely, if not actually killing the pilot. I consider this possible, as it was only the rear gunner who hit me at all, and then as he was going underneath me.

As the oil and glycol shot out over my starboard side and smoke began to pour into the cockpit I flew into the oil-fire smoke over Dunkirk for cover but when flames appeared down the fuselage I decided it was time to leave. This I did some six miles behind Dunkirk. As I floated down I gave the Belgian soldiers and peasants five minutes' simple pleasure by acting as an interesting target on which they might practise their musketry. Fortunately their skill was no greater than their intelligence, and I was finally rescued by the B.E.F.

One enthusiast even took a last shot at me while I was talking to the officer who had effected my rescue.

To understand the problem before Fighter Command one must visualize how the Germans were working their attacks.

First came a screen of fighters, Me. 109s with a stiffening of Me. 110s, stretching up to twenty thousand feet. Then came the bombers. The fighters never came by themselves, never came looking for a fight but always as an escort for the bombers, to clear the sky for them so that they could do their job. And they always came in force. There were never half a dozen bombers with a couple of fighters as an escort. They never sent less than fifteen fighters out at a time, and they frequently sent forty or more to escort sixty bombers. And they would keep up attacks on that kind of scale a dozen

times a day. It was useless, therefore, to send out our
fighters singly or in threes or sixes or even in nines. They
could never get near the German bombers like that. To
send out weak formations meant heavy losses to our
fighters as well as failure to give the troops below any
cover. The trouble was that we had too few. So if our
fighters went out in strength, as they should, the same
pilots and the same aircraft would have to go out again
later in the day. The larger the formations they went
over in the more patrols each pilot had to fly in the day
and the more tired he got. The number of fighter pilots
was limited, and the days at the beginning of June are
very long.

So the staff had to strike a balance between sending
out small formations which failed in their object and
were likely to result in heavy losses and sending out
tired men.

Then there were the aircraft to consider as well as the
pilots. If the available force could be divided into two,
each covering half the daylight hours, so that no pilot
need fly in the afternoon if he had already flown during
the morning, it meant that his aircraft could be on the
ground for overhaul and maintenance from noon to
three or four o'clock next morning. Under those conditions the aircraft could be relied upon absolutely. But
if the demands on men and machines were greater than
that and the maintenance of aircraft had to be done in

the hours of darkness the strain on them became too great and their serviceability suffered. As it was, the ground staffs of fitters, riggers, mechanics, armourers, etc., often were working for eighteen hours a day. And they worked cheerfully, giving their very best all the time. They all knew not only what their own pilots and their own squadrons were doing but how the battle with the Luftwaffe was going. They were kept informed of the progress of the battle. They knew what depended on them and they were proud of their work.

Again the staff knew very well that there is a breaking point for all men and if the pilots of a squadron got too tired that squadron had to be taken out of the battle and sent up north to one of the other groups for a week's rest. The trouble about that was that the longer a squadron stayed in the battle the more the pilots learned about air fighting and the less easily could they be spared.

We sent only our best fighters: Spitfires, Hurricanes, and the one odd squadron of a new fighter, the Boulton Paul Defiant, with an armament of four guns in a power-operated turret just behind the pilot.

The Hurricane pilots had the hardest time of it. Many of them had been through the earlier phases of the battle during the advance into Belgium and the retreat to Dunkirk. They had been exposed to anti-aircraft fire as well as meeting the German fighters. On the other hand, the Spitfire squadrons had been held in reserve and had not been used inland over France. The Spitfires were planned to be a surprise for those German pilots who pushed out over the Channel or came over to England. The Defiants, with their turret armament, were a surprise too. The Spitfires were superior to anything they came up against—in speed as well as armament and manoeuvrability. The Hurricane, on the other hand, was slower than either the Me. 109 or the Me. 110.

When big formations of our fighters went across the Channel the Spitfire squadrons would go up on top, to twenty thousand feet or so, and they would take care of the top layers of the German-fighter screen, leaving the Hurricanes and the odd squadron of Defiants to take care of the German bombers.

In dive-bombing the aircraft does a power dive on the target, during which it gets up an enormous acceleration. If it released its bombs during such a dive they would be left behind it in the air, much as torpedoes are left behind in the wake of high-speed mosquito craft when they discharge them over the stern and afterwards swerve aside. The German dive bomber does not do that. When it has reached a certain speed it puts on air brakes—metal grids under the wings. It then releases its bomb. The bomb is shot forward in the line in which the aircraft has been travelling while the aircraft slows up. At the moment of slowing up the German dive bomber offers an absolutely perfect target. On May 29 the air gunners of the squadron of twelve Defiants did great execution among German dive bombers.

From May 26 till June 4 the evacuation went on without a pause, but small parties of soldiers were still being brought off the French coasts for some days afterwards. The air battle over Dunkirk can be reckoned to have lasted from May 26 until the early morning of June 6.

By the end of that time our fighters had obtained such a superiority over the enemy that German bombers immediately jettisoned their bombs and turned tail at the sight of them. German fighters, though they still would make one dive upon a British fighter, would not return to the attack when that failed. In the final stages of the battle the Me. 109s avoided our fighters whenever possible.

In the most critical days of the battle our Spitfire pilots made as many as four patrols a day. But, in spite of such desperately hard fighting, their casualties were lighter than those of Hurricane pilots. In the battle over Dunkirk our fighters shot down 603 enemy aircraft for certain. Our losses were 130 aircraft and 120 pilots. Fighter Command had inflicted its first measured defeat on the Luftwaffe. Not only had our troops been evacuated from an almost impossible position, but the enemy had lost something like ten times as many men as we had. For it must be remembered that the majority of the

German aircraft lost carried crews of two or more. The figures given are not all the German losses during this period, for Coastal Command aircraft also took a hand in the fighting. I am not aware of the full figures of German aircraft shot down by Coastal Command aircraft and can only give as an example an air battle on the afternoon of June 1. Three United States-built Lockheed Hudsons were cruising off Dunkirk when they sighted three or four groups of enemy aircraft, each consisting of about a dozen Ju. 87s, which were attacking small boats and trawlers.

The Hudsons attacked separately and in a series of engagements drove off the German bombers, fetched a tug to take in tow two lifeboats packed with troops which had been attacked, and shot down four Ju. 87s for certain, besides damaging three others, one of them very severely. They received no damage whatever from enemy fire, although one of them had a narrow escape, since it stalled in a steep climb and only recovered at a height of a hundred feet above the water. Their victory showed how completely dependent these dive bombers were on their fighter protection. When they were caught without it they put up a very poor defense.

Again it must not be forgotten that the German aircraft were exposed to intense anti-aircraft fire and that a number must have been shot down or damaged by the navy.

THIRTY–SEVEN TO NONE

This *Defiant* Squadron accounted for thirty-seven enemy aircraft in one day without loss to itself. One air gunner alone shot down eight of the enemy in one encounter. Pilots receiving last-minute instructions and advice from the Squadron Leader.

The full German losses at Dunkirk had been very great and for their losses they had achieved but little. In Mr. Churchill's words: "There was a victory inside this deliverance which should be noted. It was gained by the Royal Air Force."

CHAPTER XII

Daylight Raids on Britain

W<small>E</small> <small>COME</small> to the "Battle of Britain," already described in a pamphlet written for the Air Ministry by a gifted writer to which I can add nothing but a few touches of emphasis which would have been out of place in an official publication. I recommend all my readers to read *The Battle of Britain* if they have not already done so.

Before describing the enemy's onslaught it would be well to consider British methods of defence. Fighter aircraft cannot always be waiting for the enemy in the air. The numbers of aircraft and of pilots and the life of engines are all too limited for the method of maintaining a continuous patrol round the British coasts to be feasible. The fighter squadrons, in different stages of preparedness, await the enemy's raids upon the ground.

The most advanced stage of preparedness, "standby,"

is with the pilots seated in the cockpits and the aircraft facing into wind. They have only to start their engines and take off. Generally the most advanced state of preparedness is "readiness," with the aircraft in position and the pilots close at hand. Then comes "advanced available," then "normal available," and then "released," in which case the pilots are free until a given hour. Finally, at every fighter aerodrome a proportion of the aircraft strength is in the hands of maintenance parties undergoing repairs, overhauls, and tests. The more actual fighting there is, and the longer it goes on, the greater is the proportion of aircraft likely to be undergoing repair.

After each sortie every aircraft needs refuelling, and if it has been in action its machine guns will need reloading.

If we consider that many of the enemy bases are in the Artois district of France, some of them only one hundred miles from London, and that the raiders travel at speeds of over 300 m.p.h. it is obvious that there is not much time to spare if British fighters are to be ordered up in time to intercept them.

The method adopted is roughly as follows: Britain is divided into a number of sectors, each with its own fighter aerodromes and headquarters, and a number of adjacent sectors are grouped together under group headquarters. The approach of the enemy becomes known by a variety of means[1]—he is seen and he is heard —and the information thus acquired is passed with all possible swiftness to operations rooms, in each of which is a controller responsible for a particular area.

The glory of the defeat of the German offensive in the summer of 1940 is usually given to our fighter pilots, and they deserve it. But fighter pilots are only the instruments of the controllers, without whom all their matchless courage and skill would have been useless, since they would never have been at the right place at the right time.

It will be remembered that *Alice through the Looking Glass* is based upon a chess problem, played by very odd pieces upon a fantastic board. The controller in operations room is playing a game more fantastic still. Compared with chess, it would be simple, were it not for the time element, and the time element is everything. Looking over his map table, the controller is provided with all possible relevant information. There is the map, the clouds, the direction and strength of the wind at various heights, the A.A. defences, and the balloon barrages. He is in touch with all his fighters by radio telephone, so that when he speaks they can all hear him and obey.

When information of a raid reaches him he has to

---

[1]The secret of radio-location has been revealed while this chapter is in the printer's hands.

calculate the direction and speed of the raiders and to order his fighters up to a point in the sky where they will be able to make an interception. Where naval and military commanders work with movements in two dimensions, he works in three dimensions. But to make one such interception is the easiest part of the fascinating game he plays for stakes of life or death, freedom or slavery. At his word squadrons of fighters move above the chequered board of Britain at 350 miles an hour, and the pieces won and lost fall flaming onto woods and fields and towns and villages below. And it is not, alas, a fantasy or dream.

The controller's real difficulty is not to intercept any particular raid. Granted time and sufficient resources, that is a feat that any intelligent person could achieve. But the men doing the job have to make instantaneous decisions, and the forces at their disposal in the summer of 1940 were small. Moreover, they knew that the enemy could go on raiding for weeks and that his object was to wear down and destroy the British fighter strength. The controller's difficulty was to diagnose the main raid of the day—for some raids were only feints to draw off his fighters—and to husband his resources so as not to be caught by a big raid when all his fighters were on the ground, refuelling and rearming, or if they were in the air when they had already expended fuel and ammunition.

The controller is not responsible for the actual fighting in the air. Once he has made his interception and his fighters report that they have sighted the enemy his voice is heard no more until the combat is over, when he may be asked to give a bearing that will bring them back to their aerodromes.

The author of *The Battle of Britain* tells us that before the war in practice exercises an average of 30-percent interceptions was thought satisfactory and that 50 per cent was very good. But in the summer of 1940 the percentage rose to seventy-five, ninety, and one hundred.

The controller of Number Eleven Group ordered up twenty-one squadrons on September 27, and each was able to report having sighted the enemy and made a successful interception. It was the high rate of interception which "made it possible for our superiority in pilots and aircraft to achieve its full effect." Indeed, it was what saved us. For the superiority of pilots and aircraft was one of quality. The numbers were the barest minimum necessary to save us from disaster. That they did so was due to the superlative skill of all ranks concerned—of the highly placed officers no less than pilots, mechanics, and armourers. The senior officers of Fighter Command saved Britain as surely as Nelson and Wellington saved her from Napoleon's projected invasion and under far more difficult conditions than have ever faced com-

manders on sea or land. The controllers remain, however, anonymous senior officers. I stress the part they
played here. So much has been rightly written of what
we owe to our fighter pilots that there is a tendency to
assume that the senior officers of the Royal Air Force
were mere spectators on the ground of a battle won by
young men of eighteen and twenty and that they took
no part in it themselves. This, as has been explained, was
not the case.

The controllers, particularly of Number Eleven
Group, which bore the brunt of the enemy attack, cannot be sufficiently honoured.

The evacuation of Dunkirk was followed by a month
of respite. While British bombers and Coastal aircraft
carried out widespread and most damaging raids on Germany and the occupied territories both by day and by
night the German air force confined itself almost ex-
clusively to night raids on a fairly small scale. Single
enemy aircraft did fly over Britain by day, but our relative immunity is shown by the fact that in one week
there was only one interception during daylight. The
enemy bomber was shot down. The night raids at this
period were on targets of military importance. Aerodromes in the eastern counties were attacked, though
practically no damage was done to them. It was obvious
from many of these raids that the enemy had great dif-

ficulty in locating targets at night, and in the majority of cases his bombs fell harmlessly at considerable distances from the places they were presumably meant for.

I remember listening to bombs dropping three miles away from the perimeter of a large military training camp, and, compared with many raids, that was a near miss. Errors of ten or fifteen miles were by no means uncommon. When navigation is as bad as that one would require other sources of information to know what the target really was.

If one has done a certain amount of flying oneself such mistakes are much easier to understand. Only those who have tried know how difficult it is to find one's way about by air and what grotesque mistakes are made even by experienced pilots during daylight. The contrast between these oddly amateur German efforts and our own bombings of Germany was absolutely astonishing.

A reason for the lull in German daylight raids was undoubtedly that time was required for the establishment and equipment of advanced bases for the German air force. As the British air force in France had discovered, French aerodromes were by no means ideal at the best of times and they had not been left as the Germans would have most wished to find them. Moreover, if the German air force was to occupy bases in northern

France in strength the existing aerodromes would need enlargement, and new landing fields would have to be laid out. Then the equipment for them had to be brought from Germany, and transport by rail at this period was probably impossible, owing to the destruction of bridges, viaducts, and permanent ways. Road transport must also have presented great difficulties at this time. There must also have been a tendency among all ranks in the German forces to relax just a little after such a tremendous victory. Preoccupations with promotions in rank and the distribution of medals must be allowed for. I believe that this delay in the invasion of Britain will be found to have cost Germany the war. Had the Germans flung every available soldier by every available means into Britain in June they would perhaps have won.

On the fourth of July, however, the German air force launched a series of greatly intensified attacks upon British shipping. On that· day two convoys off Portland were attacked with considerable success. Next day similar attacks were made off the Humber. On the seventh, eighth, and ninth there were heavy attacks off Dover and all down the Channel. The following week shipping was still being heavily attacked each day but with less success. About a dozen enemy aircraft were destroyed each day; on the tenth we got fifteen.

Naturally the defence of our convoys was not left only to our fighters. The small ships of the navy played

their part, and so did the ships which were being escorted. Coastal Command aircraft frequently lent a
hand. On July 12 a German bomber was shot down by
a couple of Ansons. German success depended upon the
speed of the attack—that is, upon surprise. As the attacks
continued they became less effective. They grew, however, to a climax, and as they increased so did the air
battles with our fighters. There were considerable
battles on July 25, 28, and 29. On August 8 the Germans lost between sixty and seventy aircraft. The
mounting losses appear to have led to a new policy. The
German air force suddenly switched from attacking
shipping to daylight raids upon our fighter aerodromes
carried out in great force. On August 12 the Kentish
aerodromes of Hawkinge, Manston, and Lympne were
attacked. On the thirteenth the attacks were further inland, and between eight hundred and a thousand German aircraft took part. That day they lost seventy-
eight aircraft, not counting about the same number
severely damaged, many of which cannot have got
home.

On the fourteenth they lost thirty-one. On August 15
over a thousand German aircraft took part in prolonged
raids all over the southern half of England, the Croydon
aerodrome being severely bombed by a bunch of dive
bombers which slipped through the defences but which
were intercepted on their way home. One hundred and

eighty German aircraft were shot down for the loss of thirty-four British fighters and seventeen pilots that day.

On the sixteenth the Germans came back again and that day lost seventy-five aircraft, at a cost of twenty-two British fighters and eight pilots. In six days the German air force had lost four hundred and eighty-seven aircraft. Those are all confirmed losses, exclusive of probable losses and severely damaged aircraft.

Two days later they made their last dive-bombing assault in daylight upon our aerodromes. British fighters shot down one hundred and twenty-eight enemy aircraft, and anti-aircraft batteries brought down another twenty-five. The British loss that day was twenty-two fighters and ten pilots. These attacks taught the Germans that dive-bombing attacks by day over Britain were too costly. The attempt to wear down the British fighter squadrons had failed, and the German air force had been very severely cut up. The Germans had to change their tactics.

An astonishing feature of these attacks on aerodromes was that the enemy did so little damage. They had naturally made a very considerable mess: hangars, administrative buildings, and living quarters were burned out and wrecked; there were a number of casualties, and a lot of people lost their kit. But the number of our aircraft destroyed was small and as the attacks went on it dropped to none. In the last week of the attacks we lost no aircraft upon the ground.

During one raid upon an aerodrome in the south the Germans lost as many aircraft as they had destroyed on the ground during the worst week of their raiding. The total losses of our operational aircraft were so small that one can say that the daylight attacks on aerodromes were more expensive and less effective than any operation the German air force had so far undertaken. It is obvious that this fortunate result was not only due to our fighter pilots but to all ranks. The ground staffs must have displayed most remarkable ingenuity, adaptability, and fertility of ideas. It is not by the application of a stereotyped formula that such dangers are surmounted but by widespread originality and general resourcefulness.

After the very severe defeats of August 15 and 18 enemy tactics changed again, and dive-bombing was, for the time being, abandoned. Night raids over Britain were greatly intensified, but the daylight raids went on, two to five hundred aircraft coming over every day. The majority of these were fighters, as the Germans were giving their bombers more and more protection. On August 24 big daylight raids were made on aerodromes in the southwest, and the Germans lost fifty aircraft, forty of which fell to our fighters. That night the Germans launched their first bombing raid on London.

Soon after this a new method was tried of eluding

our fighters by scattering the attackers all over the country. On September 7, in the late afternoon, an attack was made in great force on both banks of the Thames, on East London, and the London Docks. It was followed by a night raid on the same area, and the two combined were far more successful than anything the German air force had carried out over Britain. Gigantic fires were started all along the water fronts, and great damage was done in the London Docks. Thousands of the poorest people in London were rendered homeless, and hundreds were killed and severely injured. The great attack on London had begun. The German air force had a target it could not miss.

But the Germans lost one hundred and three aircraft that day. Our fighters maintained their ascendancy by day, but we had no effective answer to night bombing, except to increase the number of barrage balloons and anti-aircraft guns. Our barrage was greatly reinforced after a few days.

On September 11 the Germans made another large-scale attack and lost eighty-four aircraft shot down by our fighters and nine from anti-aircraft fire. On September 15 the biggest daylight attack of all was launched on London. Over five hundred bombers and fighters came during the morning and afternoon, and the biggest air battle of the war resulted. There is no doubt that this attack was intended to be followed by invasion.

During this battle the British fighter pilots surpassed themselves, and there has never been such a slaughter in the air. The official figure of the German losses, issued shortly afterwards, is 185 aircraft shot down. The Royal Air Force lost twenty-five aircraft and eleven pilots. It was the biggest of their victories.

The Germans made two more big daylight raids, but neither of them was on a comparable scale. On September 27 they sent over eight or nine hundred aircraft and lost one hundred and thirty-three. The Royal Air Force lost thirty-four aircraft and seventeen pilots.

September 28 was remarkable because the Royal Air Force losses were higher than the German: seven aircraft and seven pilots as against six of the enemy.

On September 30 the Germans made their last big daylight raid, sending over some six hundred aircraft. Their losses were forty-nine to the Royal Air Force twenty-two and ten pilots.

One of the main causes of the failure of the German day bombers was lack of armour. It is also almost certain that the German air·force had underestimated the British fighter strength.

If the Germans had the geographical advantage in night-bombing operations, the Royal Air Force had the enormous advantage of fighting over its own bases by day. The position at Dunkirk was reversed. Not only were large numbers of our pilots· able to bale out and resume fighting in the next day or two but a considerable number of damaged British fighters were repairable and were soon back in the fighting line.

British fighter squadrons had to draw heavily upon their reserves, but by the middle of October the Royal Air Force had more squadrons in the front line than during the first week in August.

During October and November daylight raids by the German air force became exceptional and sporadic. The attempt to destroy and overwhelm British fighter strength had been abandoned, and the invasion had been postponed.

I have given the official figures of German and British losses in some detail, but it is difficult to clothe figures with reality. One parachutist seen floating over the Sussex Weald brings more understanding than a page of statistics. One feature brought the air battles home to all in the south of England: their concentration in so small an area. The greatest number of these raids came in over the Thames or the Medway, and the battles which resulted were chiefly over Kent, Surrey, Middlesex, and Essex. The attack on London was spectacular and effective, but the effect has not proved quite what the enemy can have wished to produce by the attempt to terrorize.

So many of the inevitable sufferings of the world fall more heavily upon the poor. The German bombs rained down upon rich and poor alike. As they shattered working-class dwellings and Mayfair mansions they shattered also the ancient jealousies and suspicions of one class for another. Londoners have never been so close to one another in their sympathies as they are today. The bombs have broken the barriers of caste. What is true of London is, by all reports, true of the other great cities which have suffered. This fellow-feeling was not the result of the war but of the German bombing and it spread rapidly when the damage to the East End was followed by successive attempts to bomb Buckingham Palace. For some obscure reason the Nazis wished to kill the king and queen!

There is no possible doubt that the attacks on Buckingham Palace were deliberate, in spite of subsequent German denials. The first attack was made on September 13 about nine o'clock in the morning by an aircraft which slipped through by taking advantage of cloud cover. One of the crowd of distinguished civil servants on the way to Whitehall told me: "We ran like stags."

Seduced by the glamour of regicide, or acting on orders, the Nazi airmen ignored not only these black-coated targets but equally important military objectives in an area which fairly bristles with them. Several of their bombs hit Buckingham Palace, damaging the chapel. The king and queen were in residence at the time. Two days later Buckingham Palace was again successfully bombed in daylight. It has been hit again since, though at night.

The bombing of Buckingham Palace was an example of the inability of German propagandists, from Ribbentrop to Lord Haw-Haw to understand British reactions. For from that moment the humblest Londoners would endure everything that the enemy might do to them with stoic patience. Hitler had tried to kill the king. After that all Londoners knew they were in the same boat and there was not a ghost of a chance of the misery and suffering of the multitude taking a revolutionary turn.

Instead of that a flame of hatred of the Nazis and an understanding of what their cruelties had brought to the peoples of Europe illuminated all classes. By its light they read the future and knew that the war would go on and they would go on suffering until all were set free and the Nazi and Fascist tyrannies were utterly overthrown.

The daylight raids, though never again attempted in the grand manner, did not stop abruptly. They slowly faded out and reappeared in new forms, only to fade out again.

One form they took was the arrival of the Italians. Bomber and fighter squadrons, based in northern France, were sent by Mussolini so that the Italian air force might share in the destruction of London before it was too late and there was nothing left for them to bomb.

The Italians were first identified in late October off the south coast but they were not intercepted. Contact was first made on November 11, Armistice Day, and then again on November 23. Curiously enough, Mussolini had not sent his latest fighters but C.R. 42 biplanes, which are the counterpart of the British Gloster Gladiator. The pilot of the C.R. 42 sits in an open cockpit. The bombers were of more modern type—Fiat B.R. 20s. This is a two-engined low-winged monoplane with a top speed of 270 m.p.h., which is not bad. It has an armament of three heavy machine guns, one in a power-driven turret in the nose, one in a similar turret to the rear, and one mounted so as to fire down under the fuselage. Whatever their armament and aircraft, the Italians did not fare well. They were greeted with almost incredulous enthusiasm by the pilots of the British fighter squadron which intercepted them in the Thames estuary. In a combat lasting only a few minutes they shot down seven of the bombers and six of the fighters, with no loss to themselves.

On November 23 the surviving Italians made their second appearance and lost seven aircraft, and again there was no British loss. After that they were seen no more and some time afterwards they went home.

One of the bombers brought down carried a crew of six who were armed with bayonets and contained a bottle of Chianti, a fine Parmesan cheese, and a cheese grater. However much one may loathe Mussolini and the gangster method of government he invented, one cannot help loving the Italians as a race. Since the steady succession of defeats they have suffered in Libya, Albania, East Africa, Somaliland, and Abyssinia the Italians are becoming more popular. If out of the first hundred thousand prisoners captured by General Wavell several thousands of Italian peasants are sent to England to do farm work it seems likely that there will be as warm relations between Britain and the new Italian democracy which will arise after the war as there were when Garibaldi liberated and united the Italian people.

We are rather bad haters and while we are at war with the Nazis we have no hate to spare for the Italians. The Chianti flask and the Parmesan in that wrecked airplane went to our hearts.

November 1940 was full of remarkably clear days with cloudless skies in the south of England, and these cloudless days tempted the German air force to execute a new form of daylight raid harmless in result but annoying to Fighter Command and difficult to deal with. Only high-speed German aircraft took part and they came across the south coast at great altitudes and usually remained high, often as high as thirty thousand feet.

Aircraft at high altitude under certain weather conditions leave a trail of white vapour behind them. The explanation usually given of this is that the variation of pressure caused by the airscrew causes water in the atmosphere to condense into cloud form. It was possible for the population of Kent and East Sussex to watch these high-flying raiders from start to finish, owing to their leaving these white trails. With binoculars one could just see the aircraft forming the apex of each white trail. Sometimes it was one, sometimes it was a formation of three. As the raiders approached one saw the white lines being ruled swiftly in precise parallels from the south towards the north or northwest. Then one would catch sight of another smaller bunch of lines, like white needles, approaching at an angle as though to meet the first. Just before the intersection should have taken place the larger group would swerve away; the others would fall in behind them, and then in a few minutes the whole sky would be crisscrossed with curves and flourishes as complicated as specimens of eighteenth-century caligraphy.

The end of the raid was always the same: the great party had broken up into scattered groups, often of two or three, pursued by one a little way behind them, which were lost to sight heading away to the south across the Channel.

Sometimes quite large numbers of enemy aircraft were

involved in these invasions of the British substratosphere. One I watched on November 30 lasted several hours. New parties of enemy aircraft kept arriving in formation from the south and being broken up. Every now and then a Spitfire would come past at a lower level on its way to refuel and rearm. The sky was tangled with coils of the thin white vapour which broadened out into streaks like diaphanous baby riband and grew into a general cloud where it was blown away into the far distances. Five enemy aircraft were destroyed that day. The Royal Air Force lost two fighters, but both pilots escaped safely by parachute.

These high-level raids were difficult to intercept, so, though the Germans gained little by them, they lost few aircraft during them. Beginning in November, they continued on clear days until about the middle of December and then faded out. There have been a few more of them, though not on a big scale, during March 1941.

Raids by single enemy aircraft during daylight have occurred on most days somewhere or other in Great Britain. One day in March 1941 I watched one of these with considerable surprise because the raider was only a few hundred feet up. It was apparently a Heinkel 111 which had come out of low cloud and circled two or three times round a valley which divides the South Downs and allows a stream dignified with the title of a river to reach the sea.

The course of the raider was followed by heavy machine-gun fire, first on our side of the valley, then on the far side and back again. A moment or two later I saw it leave the valley, flying well below the top of the Downs (500 feet), and make off towards a large south-coast residential town. Machine-gun fire marked out its course after it had disappeared from view, and then two lots of bombs fell. Five minutes later the "All Clear" went.

There appeared two explanations of this piece of audacity which is the first low-level attack the enemy has made in this part of Sussex since last August. One is that the Heinkel had got into difficulties in cloud and did not wish to go back into it. The other is that the proximity of low cloud tempted the pilot to take liberties.

On May 8, 1941, daylight raids over the southeast of England were once more on a considerable scale, and ten enemy aircraft were shot down by our fighters, two others being destroyed by anti-aircraft fire. As the German air force had lost twenty-four aircraft, a record number later beaten, during raids the previous night, they may have decided that daylight raids could not be much more expensive.

CHAPTER XIII

Invasion Ports and Submarine Bases

Rᴇᴀᴅᴇʀs of that fascinating story, *The Riddle of the Sands*, by Erskine Childers, which appeared in 1908, will remember how a German invasion of England was to be carried out by the transport of an army in barges assembled secretly in the shallow channels behind the Frisian Islands and towed across the North Sea by tugs.

The occupation of Holland, Belgium, and France had shortened the distance that such invaders would have to travel by sea. The German army could invade Britain by the route twice successfully traversed by Caesar and later by William of Normandy. Their method, brought up to date and supplemented, was essentially the same and at present the only one.

Troop-carrying aircraft would, I suppose, be employed much as in the conquest of Holland, but tanks, artillery, and munitions for an army cannot be carried by air on a sufficient scale. The first wave of airborne troops would have to be followed quickly by others brought across the sea in ships. The first sign of preparations for an invasion was therefore likely to be in the collection of shipping necessary for such transport of troops and of supplies. In the first week of July 1940 British aircraft observed and photographed the massing of barges in Dutch and Belgian canals leading to the coast. Shipping was observed being brought round the coast to the Channel ports. A striking example of German thoroughness was revealed by some of the photographs of these barge concentrations. They showed barges packed side by side, lying end on to the dock side of a French port, with gangways leading on board. The odd thing was that these gangways were quite twice as long as appeared necessary. A moment's reflection shows that, though a very long gangway is unnecessary for embarkation from a quay side, it may be very useful, indeed, for disembarkation onto an open beach. The long gangways were for landing their troops, perhaps at low tide or over mud banks.

Naturally the Germans were not allowed to make all their preparations unmolested, and during the weeks following and from that time on for many months Coastal Command aircraft attacked German concentrations of barges wherever seen. Besides barges, all types of ships were being collected in what came to be known as the "invasion ports" of Ostend, Zeebrugge, Dunkirk, Calais, Boulogne, Dieppe, Havre, and Brest. On these fierce attacks were made throughout the summer and autumn both by Coastal and Bomber Command aircraft. Again and again these attacks, launched by day under cover of cloud and by night bombers, caused great fires in the docks and warehouses and in the shipping alongside. On one occasion a bombardment from ships of the British fleet brought the almost mechanical answer of the Flak anti-aircraft barrage. The bursting shells from the ships' guns had been mistaken for bombs, and the German shore batteries did not open fire until our ships had withdrawn and the bombardment was over.

Air Ministry bulletins have been reticent about the results of our attacks on the invasion ports during July, August, and September, and rumour has been particularly active upon the subject. I can therefore only say that I have seen it stated frequently that the German invasion was planned to coincide with the bombing of London on September 15 and that our attacks on the invasion ports were so destructive that the plan had to be postponed. No doubt the fact that far heavier losses appeared inevitable, had the invasion been launched, since British fighter strength had not been broken, was also a most important factor in the German decision. It is said that, owing to our bombardment, there were thirty thousand casualties among the troops assembled at the invasion ports or already embarked for the invasion. The story that large numbers of bodies in German military uniform had been washed up on the British coasts was widely reported and believed. I have no evidence for this, and it must be remembered that a dozen bodies washed ashore would create a great impression and give rise to stories of thousands.

Bombing attacks were by no means the only weapon employed by the Royal Air Force against the invader. Plans for laying mines by our aircraft, particularly in narrow waters where shipping is most concentrated, had been worked out by the Air Staff long before the Germans began using Hitler's "secret weapon," the magnetic mine. The opportunities for such mine laying had grown enormously since the German victories in the West, and on every suitable night our mine-laying aircraft went out to deposit their mines in harbours, estuaries, coastal waters, and the channels chiefly used in the water transport of enemy supplies—in fact, wherever they might prove most damaging to the enemy. Mine laying from the air needs extremely accurate navigation. Often it is only a matter of yards whether a mine falls in the fairway or into a mudbank where it will be harmless. And one tidal reach looks surprisingly like another on a dark night. Fortunately the Coastal Command had a very experienced lot of navigators from which to pick the men for this new branch of their work.

The most important part of mine laying, after accuracy in navigation, is that the aircraft should be unobserved. A silent approach, with engines throttled back, on a moonlit but cloudy night, with a good deal of wind to carry away the noise of the engines, is probably what mine-laying aircraft find best. But no doubt they can carry on in practically any weather and make a point of revisiting every area directly there is photographic evidence of mine sweeping having been carried out in it.

Naturally British attacks upon the invasion ports and mine laying in channels used by enemy shipping did not come to an end as the likelihood of invasion receded during the winter months. Such attacks are carried out frequently sometimes at night, sometimes by day, and by very varying numbers of aircraft. Sometimes waves of our aircraft will pound away all through the hours of darkness, dropping high-explosive bombs into fires earlier raiders have started along the docks and in the railway yards of a channel port. Watchers on the English coast have often seen the glow of great fires, have watched the German anti-aircraft shells winking in the sky, and have heard the thudding of our bombs.

And then one morning a solitary Blenheim will sweep over one of the invasion ports at a height of one hundred feet and, with all its machine guns blazing, will dive almost onto the heads of a battalion of German soldiers drilling on the barrack square, leaving it two or three seconds later with a swathe of dead and wounded men stretched across it and hundreds still running for the edges after the danger has passed them by.

As the likelihood of invasion diminished a new danger arose farther to the south on the French Atlantic coast, for the Germans were making a new, more successful attack upon British shipping by means of collaboration between their submarines and ocean-going aircraft, chiefly of the four-engined Focke-Wulf Condor and Kurier types.

The submarines are, for the most part, small short-range craft based on the French Atlantic ports, Brest, Quiberon, Lorient, and St. Nazaire. The aircraft are also based not far from the French coast, and both submarine bases and airfields have been very frequently and very heavily attacked.

There appeared to be a definite correlation between such heavy attacks by us early in the new year and a series of weeks which followed in which British shipping losses were below the average.

Equally important in nipping enemy plans in the bud was a night bombing raid on Bremen early in March 1941, in which the Focke-Wulf aircraft factory is reported to have been almost completely destroyed.

Many night raids were directed against the German battle cruisers *Scharnhorst* and *Gneisenau* which had slipped out into the Atlantic and were located sheltering in Brest harbour. Direct hits were scored, and among the early casualties appears to have been the German admiral, a notorious U-boat commander in the last war, whose death on active service was announced by the German wireless shortly afterwards.

The experience of Bomber Command sweeps in Heligoland Bight and of Coastal Command attacks on shipping in the North Sea and, still more, the enemy attacks upon British shipping and the British fleet showed the present limitations of aircraft when employed against heavily armoured ships.

Bombing and machine-gun attacks even upon unarmed and unarmoured vessels, lightships, and fishing trawlers by enemy aircraft by no means always prove successful. To take a recent example: A German aircraft attacked an unarmed Brazilian cargo ship in the eastern Mediterranean for an hour and a half on March 25, 1941. The German aircraft dropped four bombs, machine-gunned the ship and her crew and her boats after she had hove to, in spite of two large Brazilian flags painted on her sides and the waving of the white flag. Two of the crew were killed and several wounded, some seriously, but the German raider failed to sink the ship which was later brought into Alexandria under her own power. Yet the aircraft had complete leisure in which to carry out the attack.

Enemy aircraft have frequently been brought down by British trawlers armed only with Lewis guns. And attacks on vessels of the British fleet have proved extremely costly to both the German and the Italian air forces. Indeed, few warships, exclusive of submarines, have been sunk by aircraft during the present war except when they have managed to make a surprise attack, have attacked in very large numbers, or have used torpedoes.

A ship cannot be sunk by damage, however severe, above the water line, and a heavily armoured ship is unlikely to have a hole knocked in her hull below water level by a bomb. The torpedo is a far more deadly weapon, and much more damage has been done to enemy shipping since Coastal Command aircraft have taken to using it, and the losses of the attacking aircraft have been much less.

If the bomb be represented by the point on which it drops the torpedo would be represented by a line. Mathematically a point on the surface of the sea is defined by two variables and a line by only one. The possibilities of error in aiming are therefore halved against a stationary target. Against this enormous advantage, the bomb can cause damage by a near miss; the torpedo has to hit. Moreover, the bomb cannot be avoided; the torpedo, which takes a considerable time to reach its target, can frequently be avoided if it is seen in time.

One great advantage of the torpedo over the bomb is in the method of delivery. The torpedo carrier must be low down on the horizon, as torpedoes are best dropped from just above the surface, though they may be dropped from as much as 50 feet. The attacking aircraft is less distinctly seen and can keep at a greater range, and the attack may be made, unsuspected by the victim. The bomber makes its attack in full view overhead. The torpedo carrier is therefore far less likely to be damaged by retaliatory fire. Most important of all, the torpedo hits its mark below the water line.

The use of the torpedo by aircraft is no new thing. It was first conceived of by Admiral Murray Sueter. In March 1914 Squadron Commander Longmore, until recently commanding the Royal Air Force in the Middle East, gave a display of torpedo dropping from a Sopwith seaplane before Mr. Winston Churchill, then First Lord of the Admiralty. During the first air-naval manoeuvres a few years before the present war some sensation was caused in naval circles when H.M.S. *Warspite* was hit by six torpedoes from the air.

The attack on the Italian fleet by Swordfish torpedo-carrying aircraft of the Fleet Air Arm in the harbour of Taranto on a moonlight night will be forever the classic example of the successful use of the torpedo by aircraft. A comparatively small number of obsolescent aircraft, which suffered minor loss, achieved a naval victory which resulted in an alteration of the whole balance of sea power in the Mediterranean.

CHAPTER XIV

The Night Bombing

THERE ARE SEVERAL sides of the air war with which I have been able to deal fairly fully, but some cannot be thus dealt with, and of one or two subjects of great importance I have intentionally omitted all mention whatever. For the war is in progress, and all information published and thus given to the enemy has to be most carefully scrutinized.

Unfortunately for the armchair critic of the war, many of its most vital aspects are on the border line of what may be discussed. Nothing would be more illuminating as to the way the war is going and nothing would be more heartening to the adherents of the democracies than a full and detailed comparison of the results of German and British night bombing raids. Unfortunately there are few things the enemy more desires to know than precisely what military damage he has inflicted on British war industry. It is impossible, therefore, to do more than discuss British and German bombing policies and their results in very general terms.

It is a great pity that details must not be given, since the public knows well enough the damage to civilian life and property and knows, too, that the British bombing force is considerably smaller than the German and that it is operating under great geographical disadvantages. It is therefore naturally prone to conclude that the damage done to the German war effort by the Royal Air Force bears no comparison with that inflicted on our war effort by the enemy. That is what one would naturally expect. It is, I believe, the reverse of the truth. British raids on Germany have done more damage to the German war effort than German raids have done to the British.

Everyone would have expected the British fighter strength to have been overwhelmed by the German attack during July, August, and September, but we have seen that British fighter squadrons inflicted casualties of four or five to one on the enemy measured in aircraft and very much more measured in terms of personnel. That victory would not be believed if we had not the figures before us and many independent sources of evidence to confirm it. Its results are known and accepted partly because the daylight raids were fought out over

Britain and the results in crashed enemy aircraft were obvious to newspaper reporters and to the population. The battle went on over our heads, and it was impossible that we should not know, roughly, the result.

Nothing is seen of our raids on Germany, except occasionally in photographs, and no figures can be given for the comparative results, and even comparisons of what is intended by the raids are difficult. British raids on Germany are part of one plan; the German raids show evidence of several different plans.

But to take the British raids first: The British raids are the fruit of study of the German war industry. The plan for a "strategic offensive" can be regarded in one way as an extension of the effects of the blockade and in another as a "war in depth." In preparation for the war Germany laid in great stocks of those essentials which she cannot obtain in sufficient quantities within her borders or from her neighbours in Europe.

The British Ministry of Economic Warfare studies the situation of Germany with regard to all such stocks, and the British bombing raids are planned by the British Air Ministry in conjunction with the Ministry of Economic Warfare. For example, Germany is short of oil, lubricants, rubber, and chrome. These, then, are not only objects of special attention to our blockade, but the stocks of them in Germany are targets of the first importance. Particularly vulnerable is oil.

Oil stocks at Rotterdam, oil refineries at Hamburg and Bremen, synthetic-oil-hydrogenation plants at Gelsenkirchen in the Ruhr, at Pollitz near Stettin, at Leuna near Leipzig have been bombed and bombed and bombed, and their production has been stopped for periods of a week at a time and their output permanently diminished.

Probably the second most important target is transport. The German railway system is heavily overworked and continually breaking down. It has been maintained by such hand-to-mouth expedients as commandeering the rolling stock from occupied countries and even from neutrals who never get railway wagons back once they have gone into Germany. These expedients have in themselves made German problems of supply and of trade far more acute.

The Royal Air Force persistently attacks the great German marshalling yards, railway stations, bridges, and viaducts. The underground system in Berlin was put out of action for some time.

Other forms of transport attacked are canals and inland ports, such as those at Mannheim, Cologne, and Duisburg Ruhrort.

Factories are the next target. In the selection of the targets of most importance in the manufacture of munitions there is room for considerable subtlety.

Before 1914 Britain and France had relied on im-

FULL MOON RAIDERS

A bomber crew entering their plane as the moon is rising. This photograph was taken at the base of one of the Night Bomber Squadrons engaged in the attack, immediately before the crew left on their moonlight trip.

porting German magnetos. As a result their manufacture of airplanes and cars would have come to a standstill if they had not been able to import magnetos from the United States and hastily to set about manufacturing magnetos themselves. All equipment for war today is similarly dependent upon assembling a host of different parts separately manufactured. If the production of one item is knocked out all the rest are useless. Destroy the magneto factories, and the factories building the other components of tanks, motorcars, and aircraft are useless.

The British bombing attacks have been made on this selective plan of knocking out the weakest link in the chain of manufacture. There are two advantages in this. The first is its economy. If you can hold up production in twenty factories by destroying one of them you can use the bombers which would have been used to bomb the other nineteen to attack other targets and spread paralysis in other industries. The other is that you put a very large number of men out of work. To keep the nineteen factories working at full pressure would result in production getting completely out of step. And that is what is happening to production in Germany today.

Germany is an immensely strong industrial country with a very hard-working, disciplined population. What the Royal Air Force destroys the Germans, working in night and day shifts, repair and rebuild. But a continu-

ally increasing part of the German war effort is occupied solely with repairs, with starting wheels which
have stopped turning.

And increasing numbers of German workmen have
to be transferred hastily from jobs which have been rendered redundant to those which have suddenly become
desperately urgent.

It will be asked, "How does this plan of crippling
German war production differ from German plans of
doing exactly the same to England?"

The answer is that it does differ rather surprisingly.
The Germans no doubt have made a similar survey of
British war industries and have set out to destroy those
which are most important. But they started after the
British; their bombing is not so accurate, and they have
had so many other plans of bringing Britain down that
they have not concentrated on war industries in the
same way. Their blockade of Britain by sea is far less
effective than the British blockade of Germany, and
they cannot prevent the flow of troops from the British
colonies or of munitions from the United States. Royal
Air Force pilots, both British and colonial, are being
increasingly trained in Canada, where the aircraft they
fly, the food they eat, and the fuel they burn are all
completely out of reach of the German bomber and the
German submarine. With the passing of the Lease and
Lend Act, an increasingly large portion of British muni-

tions will be manufactured where Germany cannot interfere—except by conspiracy and sabotage.

Perhaps owing to these inevitable limitations, Germany's attacks upon British industry have been far less scientific and much more aimed at the morale of the people than at the bench and the lathe.

This is not to minimize the results of German bombing on British war industry. It has been tremendous—at moments.

Yet in spite of these attacks British aircraft production has gone up steadily since the present government came into office.

Lord Beaverbrook, until lately Minister of Aircraft Production, has told us that the methods which prevented the enemy's attacks upon our aerodromes from doing much damage to aircraft on the ground have been adopted in our munition and aircraft factories. In a speech during April he stated that one famous aircraft manufactory was now located in forty-two separate works scattered over four different counties.

The main German objective has definitely become the civil population, particularly that of the larger towns. London is the ideal target for Goering's Luftwaffe. Its strong points were not night flying, or navigation, so it was important that it should be given an objective which it could not miss.

The number of casualties rose to a peak at the end of

September, and the population, particularly the very poor, took to spending the nights in the London tubes. The conditions in the inadequate shelters which had been provided up till then became appalling, and it was not until Mr. Herbert Morrison became Home Secretary in place of Sir John Anderson that the work of cleaning up the shelters and putting sleeping bunks onto the underground-railway platforms was tackled.

There was never any danger of the cockney's morale giving out. The danger was that lack of sleep and the difficulties of life would exhaust the population to such a point that the output of industry would drop. How far such a drop occurred in greater London during these months I do not know, but I believe any decline owing to general fatigue was more than offset by the angry determination to "beat Hitler."

The "blitz," as the long-drawn-out pounding of London came to be called, certainly made Londoners determined to go on with the war till the end. In a curious way it made the war far more popular. Everyone saw that winning it was a matter of life or death, and life is always popular with those who have met with a nasty but not mortal accident.

Heroism and self-sacrifice, as one would expect, were found to the degree in which they were needed. They are qualities latent in the vast majority of normal human beings and appear to suit the environment. The blitz made courage necessary to most normal men and women. For one thing, it made life so much more agreeable. Perhaps the most unexpected result of the bombing is a decrease in crime.

In October 1940 the outlook was grim. It seemed reasonable to suppose that, having launched their attack upon the civil population, the Germans would put all their energies into night raids. Their losses at that period from British anti-aircraft fire were negligible, and our night fighters had failed to bring down any raiders. The long nights were before us, and there seemed no reason why the German air force should not send over waves of bombers every ten minutes from four o'clock in the afternoon till eight o'clock next morning. But instead of the German attack increasing it declined, spasmodically reasserting itself, and slowly faded through the winter months. It was not until March, when the long nights were over and the equinox was at hand, that heavy raids began again, and by that time Fighter Command had a body of trained night fighter pilots who had developed a new technique. During the first big raid on London in March our night fighter pilots accounted for nine enemy aircraft. The following night the German bombers visited Merseyside and lost five aircraft to our night fighter pilots, flying the new Bristol Beaufighter. In the raid on London "other devices" accounted for one or two other enemy aircraft.

About this time British fighter pilots began to go over to enemy aerodromes in the north of France when the German night bombers would be likely to be taking off or to be returning after a raid. Several enemy bombers were shot down in this way; others were machine-gunned as they taxied out or in on the ground.

Why had the German air raids decreased through the winter months when the opposite might have been expected?

There are rival theories for this decline. During February the British public was warned by the Air Ministry not to rejoice too soon over the decline in the blitz and that it was merely due to bad weather conditions.

The aerodromes used by the German air force in the north of France are rather small, and northern France is particularly liable in winter to those thick ground fogs which go with hard frosts and which leave every twig and blade of grass coated with white whiskers of rime. Such fogs come down or rise from rivers and low-lying ground with great rapidity. There is every probability that the German night bombers have had a high rate of wastage.

It is not generally realized how high this may be. If ground fog came down quickly while a couple of hundred German raiders were over Britain it is quite possible that forty or fifty would crash or make forced landings on their return. One or two experiences of losses on a big scale like that would make the German Air Staff very cautious.

But, apart from extremely heavy losses owing to exceptional weather, the ordinary operational losses are probably very high, according to British ideas, for the Germans are returning to rather small airfields and their aircraft were not built with night flying in view.

There is therefore an unofficial theory that the German air force has had much greater losses than the British Air Ministry is prepared to claim. According to this view, the Germans cannot risk raiding every night, as they wish to conserve their forces until they are ready for an invasion.

The explanation that the Germans were deterred from raiding in the winter months by bad weather has been borne out by the resumption of large-scale raids in March and April, when there were prevailing east winds and reliable weather.

The number of civilians killed and injured in September was 6954 and 10,615, in October 6334 and 8695, in November 4588 and 6202. The decline proceeded until February, during which month 789 were killed and 1068 were injured.

In March 4259 were killed and 5557 were injured. This figure includes the very heavy raids on Merseyside and Clydeside. In the latter area there were 1100 killed. A German pilot, giving a propaganda talk over the German wireless, is reported to have described looking down over the water and seeing docks and ships which presented a most tempting target.

"But I had other orders," he concluded.

Owing to the high death roll resulting from these "other orders," the Clydeside workers who have a reputation as "Reds" are now heart and soul in the war.

One may contrast these attacks on civilians with one of a series of repeated British raids on Kiel which took place on April 7–8, when some of the new high-power bombs were dropped. Later reconnaissance showed that the Deutschewerke shipbuilding yard, the Germania shipbuilding yard, the floating quay, and the torpedo stores had been gutted and that many submarine slipways were damaged.

The raid on London on the night of April 16–17 was extremely heavy. Waves of German bombers came over from France, probably making two trips, from shortly after dark until just before dawn. The panorama from outside London was impressive in the extreme. The flicker of exploding bombs against the sky, the hundreds of searchlights, the twinkling points of bursting anti-aircraft shells, and the slowly dropping bunches of flares are all familiar. The red glow of a bomber dropping in flames was a welcome addition.

London contains so many military objectives that no doubt several were hit. Germany can place to the credit side of such bombing raids the diversion of labour and effort not only of A.R.P. and fire-fighting services but of demolition squads and the hundreds of men engaged in building repairs and the restoration of supplies of water, gas, and electricity, some of whom might otherwise have been employed in making munitions. But the damage to civilian property is spread on so many shoulders that it interferes to a surprisingly small extent with the business of government and our preparedness for war.

One of the most dangerous results of the renewed night raids is, in my opinion, the demand in the newspapers for reprisals. Angry and ignorant critics demand that the Air Staff should interrupt a carefully planned program of scientific destruction calculated to cripple Germany's war effort and should "bomb for panic," apparently on the grounds that the German people lack the stamina shown not only by the British but by the Chinese, the Finns, and many other peoples. Such demands appear to me hysterical and inopportune. So long as the Royal Air Force has a far smaller force of bombers at its disposal than the G.A.F. and they are operating under geographical disadvantages which make large pay loads of bombs impossible it appears to me foolish to waste bombs on civilians rather than on aircraft factories and submarine assembly yards. For bombing to be effective against civilians it must inspire abject terror and despair. This the bombing of cities has failed to do except where the people are war-weary and hungry. I can conceive that in 1943, when Britain has achieved a tremendous air superiority, the ruthless bombing of the war-weary population of Germany on a far more gigantic scale than has been experienced by any British city may well be the most effective way to bring about a German revolution. By butchering the German population indiscriminately it might be possible to goad them into a desperate rising in which every member of the Nazi party would have his throat cut. To "bomb for panic" now could have no such effect, while it would give the German rulers a golden opportunity to complete preparations for invasion or to win the battle of the Atlantic.

There is, however, a distinct hope that the Royal Air Force may before long render night raiding a much more expensive business for the Germans than it has proved hitherto.

The following figures have been issued by the Air Ministry for German losses at night during raids on Britain.

January   15. Highest number in one night 5.
February 15. Highest number in one night 3.
March   47. Highest number in one night 13.
April   90. Highest number in one night 13.
Seven nights of May 74.
                    Highest number in one night 24.

Of the number brought down on the night of May 7–8 twenty fell to night fighters, three to anti-aircraft fire, and one to the balloon barrage. On the night of May 11, that of the full moon, all records were beaten, and thirty-two bombers were shot down by our night fighters during a heavy raid on London.

The rapid increase of German raiders shot down shows that some solution of the problem of the night raider is at hand. The enemy have not yet had equal luck or developed equal skill. On the night of May 7–8 widespread raids were made by Bomber Command, including heavy raids on Brest, during which the *Scharnhorst* and *Gneisenau* battle cruisers each received direct hits. Two British aircraft were lost during these operations.

The Douglas D.B. 7, to which I shall refer later, is now being extensively employed as a night fighter, in which capacity it is known as the Havoc. It is an extremely manoeuvrable medium bomber and is one of the many American-built aircraft giving extremely good service. The tactics of night fighting is not a subject for discussion in print. All that can be said is that it is best carried out by an aircraft with more endurance, range, and reserves of ammunition than the single-seater. The longer it can stay up the better, and the more ammunition it carries the more aircraft it may be able to account for during one night. Several of our night fighter pilots have bagged two enemy bombers during a night more than once.

Thus there is every reason to feel that by the time the short summer nights are lengthening German night raiders will be paying a very high price for their activities.

One of the fruitful ways of dealing with the night raider is to catch him taking off from or returning to his base. Several of our Havocs have caught the enemy out in this way and on occasion have shot down Messerschmitts sent up to attack them.

CHAPTER XV

The Mediterranean Campaigns

THE MEDITERRANEAN and Middle East campaigns are entering upon a critical second phase as I write during May 1941. Detailed information is not available about them, and they can only be treated in the broadest outline.

British operations have been rendered possible and continuously assisted by sea power, and the handling of the fleet in the Mediterranean has revived the greatest glories of the British navy. There was nothing in the war of 1914–18 comparable with these daring and difficult operations. In the Great War the navy made mistakes which sometimes proved extremely expensive. For example, on the outbreak of war, the German battleship *Goeben* and the cruiser *Breslau* were allowed to enter the Dardanelles, where they played a considerable part in bringing Turkey into the war against us.

This time there have been no naval blunders and but few naval misfortunes, while again and again there have been actions which have revealed daring and genius of the first order.

Nowhere have such actions been more frequent than in the Mediterranean. From the very beginning of their entry into the war the Italians have been reluctant to face the British navy. On the rare occasions when the Italian fleet has been intercepted it has sought to break off action and has fled. Yet at the beginning it was considerably superior to the British forces which could be spared, for the British were forced by the mere facts of geography to divide their naval forces, maintaining one fleet based on Alexandria and another based on Gibraltar. The Italian fleet was therefore in a strong strategical position, and it was a matter of the first importance to reduce its strength, particularly as there were two new 35,000-ton battleships building in Italian yards.

No counteroffensive to the threatened Italian invasion of Egypt from Libya could be carried out unless the army engaged on it was free from any anxiety about an Italian naval attack on its lines of communication along the Egyptian coast.

An incident early in the war with Italy showed that Britain was likely to receive assistance from unexpected quarters. On July 9, 1940, the Italian battleship *Cesare* was mistaken for H.M.S. *Hood* by Italian aircraft and so severely damaged during their bombing attacks that she only reached Genoa with difficulty. The incident was adjusted on land, where the Italian navy and air force could meet as man to man. Outnumbered by the sailors, the Italian pilots were chased round the town with knives.

Several deductions can be drawn from this action. The most important perhaps is that Italian naval anti-aircraft fire was not of the first quality.

The strategic importance of Malta is a factor of first-class importance in the Mediterranean. It is the link between East and West.

Malta is fifty miles from the Sicilian coast and about two hundred from the Italian colony of Tripolitania. It lies right in the path of Italian communications with her African colonies. Had the Italians captured Malta they would indeed have made the Mediterranean their own sea. They could then more easily have stopped the passage of British convoys through the Mediterranean and have made the passage of warships hazardous.

Malta, however, is strongly held, and though there have been large numbers of raids upon it they have not weakened the British defences. No attempt to capture Malta was made by the Italians, and the moment for it may have passed now that their fleet has been defeated.

Yet it is difficult to understand why they did not try or get the Germans to try for them with airborne troops.

The first step in the capture of Malta would have been to secure mastery of the air. British fighter squadrons at Malta had, therefore, much the same part to play, on a small scale, as those of Fighter Command in Britain, and events ran much the same course. Italian raids began early in June 1940 but were not effective. Three German Heinkels were identified early in June, but the crews may have been Italian, and German air cooperation was not available on a big scale until German dive bombers and fighters were based in large numbers in Sicily. The attacks on Malta then became intense, but German losses were so severe that large-scale attacks have been intermittent. Mr. Churchill announced in a speech in February that the Germans had lost fifty aircraft in one attack on Malta. Forty others were destroyed on the ground at their air base at Catania about the same time. This figure rather suggests that the aerodrome was congested and that the German air force in Italy was suffering, much as the British air forces in France had done, from a lack of satellite landing grounds. The ground defences at Malta are stated to be greater than in any equal area of the British Empire.

The possibility of invading islands would seem to depend on the capacity of the attacker to obtain complete air supremacy in order to land airborne troops, both parachutists and from troop carriers. The Italians were not in a position to make such an attempt on Malta, nor did the British make any attempt on Pantellaria or the Dodecanese Islands, though the advantages of capturing them are obvious.

The German invasion of Crete is proceeding while I write. The novel feature which has been announced is the transport of troops by glider, on the Russian model. Very large numbers of parachutists, dressed in British battledress, are reported to have been employed. Whether the operations on Crete prove successful or not, we must regard them as likely to continue. The Germans do not lightly abandon their enterprises. What is being attempted in Crete will be tried again, perhaps in Cyprus, possibly in Ireland, and certainly in Britain.

The possibilities of success will depend largely on what fighter opposition they meet in the air and whether they can land tanks. Without overwhelming air superiority the advantages would appear to lie with the defence. We may be confident that such an attempt on Britain would fail.

The case of holding islands lying within a few miles of a hostile shore is a matter of far more difficulty, since they cannot get sufficient warning of air attacks which can be carried out almost without interruption. The Channel Islands, which lie just off the French coast, were evacuated partly to spare their populations the horrors of continual air bombardment, partly because of the difficulties of defending them, which would have required large numbers of anti-aircraft guns for which there was greater need in Britain. Nor was it possible, either, to improvise bases for our fighter aircraft or to spare fighter aircraft for the defence of the islands had bases existed.

British supremacy in the Mediterranean has been due almost entirely to the intelligent handling of aircraft by British naval commanders. In every big naval action naval aircraft have played an important part and at Taranto they altered the whole balance of naval power by an attack on the Italian fleet lasting a few minutes.

The aircraft taking part in these actions have been based in aircraft carriers. The Italians have none. It is therefore interesting to consider the value of aircraft carriers, against which much has been said.

A navy may have the use of aircraft without aircraft carriers. Most modern battleships and large cruisers can catapult aircraft off their decks for reconnaissance purposes but they cannot carry them in any numbers or as a powerful defensive or offensive arm. The aircraft carrier alone can carry enough fighters to protect the fleet from an enemy air attack and can bring a swarm of torpedo-carrying aircraft within striking distance of the enemy's fleet, his naval bases, and anchorages. Its aircraft can help to delay an enemy while the body of the fleet comes up.

Aircraft carriers are inevitably very large ships, as their deck serves as a runway. Their size makes them particularly vulnerable to air attack. The British navy has lost two aircraft carriers during the war, though in neither case by attack from the air. Early in the war H.M.S. *Courageous* was sunk by an enemy submarine in the English Channel. As will be remembered, H.M.S. *Glorious* was sunk off Narvik by the German battle cruisers *Scharnhorst* and *Gneisenau*. These are undoubtedly the most severe losses suffered by the British navy during the war. In each case numbers of pilots and aircraft were also lost.

Both *Ark Royal* and *Illustrious* have been damaged by air attack, and on each occasion it seemed miraculous that they escaped. The Germans were obviously in doubt for a very long time whether they had sunk *Ark Royal* or not. In the hopes of finding out, they made the sinking of the ship one of the chief items of their wireless talks and propaganda. For months they reiterated the parrot question, "Where is the *Ark Royal?*" and added taunts and jeers at the Royal Navy. The British refused to be drawn, and the question was not answered until the battle of the River Plate, when the ship was one of those which raced across the South Atlantic in case the *Graf Spee* came out from Monte Video to try and wipe out her inglorious defeat at the hands of lighter armed cruisers. Hitler preferred to scuttle.

Since then *Ark Royal* has played an important part in the western Mediterranean, her aircraft fulfilling an independent bombing attack on Leghorn during the bombardment of Genoa.

The aircraft carrier *Illustrious* also had a narrow escape when the German dive bombers established in Sicily scored a signal success over the British fleet which was engaged in passing a convoy through the Malta channel to Greece. Though the convoy got through safely, the cruiser *Southampton* was set on fire and had to be abandoned; a destroyer was sunk, and *Illustrious* received direct hits. She was able to reach Malta and after partial repairs proceeded to Alexandria under her own power.

The objection to aircraft carriers is the reasonable prejudice against putting too many eggs in one basket. It is possible that there is room for revolutionary improvements in their design. But no improvements, short of making them unsinkable, affect that argument. The other objection, of more value before the war than today, was that aircraft carriers are expensive and that when Britain was short of aircraft millions of pounds were swallowed up in building ships which could only carry limited numbers of aircraft. Better, it was argued, spend the money on bombers based on shore, like those of Coastal Command, than on additional aircraft carriers carrying a few hundred obsolescent types of aircraft, such as the Swordfish.

This argument has been, in reality, answered in two ways. Coastal Command of the Royal Air Force has undertaken and carried out the work which could best be performed by aircraft based on our coasts, and the aircraft carriers of the navy are being equipped with more up-to-date aircraft, such as the Roc, the Skua, and the Fulmar.

Today all arguments about the pros and cons of aircraft carriers are out of date, for the proof of the pudding is in the eating. The Admiralty policy with regard to aircraft carriers has been abundantly justified by the series of triumphs won by the Fleet Air Arm in the Mediterranean. They indeed have played the chief part in the defeat of the Italian navy. The greatest of their triumphs was the action at Taranto.

Reconnaissance aircraft of the Royal Air Force had photographed the Italian fleet in the harbour of Taranto sometime early in November. The photographs clearly showed the positions of the ships—the battleships in the outer harbour, the cruisers in the inner. Towards midnight on the night of November 11–12, 1940, the British fleet under Admiral Cunningham, with the aircraft carriers *Eagle* and *Illustrious*, reached a position within easy striking distance, for aircraft, of Taranto. It was brilliant moonlight. It was also, it is amusing to remember, a few hours after the Italian bombers and fighters based in northern France had made their inglorious attempt to bomb London.

A mixed force of Swordfish bombers and torpedo carriers with a fighter escort of Gladiators and Fulmars took off. When over Taranto harbour, which was protected by heavy ground defences and a balloon barrage, the bombers dropped parachute flares, trying to light up the target, and then dropped their bombs. Part of their object, in which they succeeded, was to draw the enemy's anti-aircraft fire and allow the torpedo carriers, which followed in waves, to get within striking distance. The attempt was successful, and the torpedo carriers came in to close range.

The total strength of the Italian battle fleet at that time was six battleships, two of the Littorio class (35,-000 tons), which had just been put into service, and four of the recently reconstructed Cavour class.

Subsequent reconnaissance showed that one of the two 35,000-ton Littorio-class battleships was knocked out. She was down by the bows, with her forecastle under water, and had a heavy list to starboard. One of the Cavour-class battleships was beached with her stern, up to and including the rear turret, under water and a heavy list to starboard. A second Cavour-class battleship was so badly damaged that she had apparently been abandoned. She had heeled over to starboard and was lying with only the forward part of her upper works above water.

In the inner harbour two cruisers were listed to starboard and were surrounded with oil fuel lying on the water. Two fleet auxiliaries were lying with their sterns under water. The pilot of the reconnaissance aircraft also reported that four "shapes" could be seen under water off the entrance to the graving dock in the inner harbour.

This major naval victory, which altered the balance of sea power in the Mediterranean, was carried out for the loss of two aircraft shot down, the crews of which were apparently taken prisoners.

The best comment on Taranto was a gibe given in one of the Free French radio broadcasts shortly afterwards. It was a definition of the word *"scaphandrier"* as *"inspecteur de la marine italienne."* A *scaphandrier* is a man wearing a diving suit.

In October Mussolini launched an attack upon Greece. Not till the following April did Germany come to the aid of her ally, and during those six months of winter the Greek army drove the invaders back into Albania and held them there.

During this period British help was limited to the air and to the provision of weapons of all kinds, chiefly captured from the Italians in Libya, and of a few experts in demolition and kindred work. The Greeks were anxious not to provoke the Germans by accepting British help on too large a scale, and for political reasons of this sort the contingent of the Royal Air Force sent to help Greece was limited not only by the number of aircraft which could be spared but also by the number of aerodromes made available.

Had it been possible to construct and equip a number of air bases in Greece before the Germans built their air bases in Bulgaria the story of the German conquest of the Balkans would have been very different.

With the consent of the Greeks a British force occupied Crete and an air base was constructed there. It may be remembered that during the war of 1914–18 the Allies had a seaplane and flying-boat base at Suda Bay in Crete.

The first squadrons of fighters and bombers sent to Greece were equipped with Gladiators and Blenheims. Their tasks were chiefly to provide air cooperation with the Greek army by driving off Italian aircraft, to carry out reconnaissance, and to prevent Italian reinforcements and supplies reaching the front. Big bombing raids were also carried out on the chief Italian supply base at Valona, ships, docks, and aerodromes being attacked. The raids on Valona were an important factor in the Albanian campaign. The succession of heavy snowstorms and exceptionally severe weather made our help in the air less effective than it would otherwise have been.

Although very greatly outnumbered, the British squadrons gained an ascendancy over the Italians. On February 28 a big air battle was fought out, British fighter squadrons bringing down twenty-six Italian aircraft.

After the earthquake at Larissa British bombers were used to fly medical supplies to the area.

During March Berat, Valona, and Durazzo were heavily raided many times. British fighters shot down eighty-five enemy aircraft during the month, and eleven were destroyed on the ground.

This brings us to the German invasion of Jugoslavia, but we must turn back to operations in North Africa, the progress of which are intimately linked up with those in Greece.

The campaign in Libya opened on December 7, 1940. General Sir Archibald Wavell's conquest of Libya was rendered possible by reinforcements of armoured and mechanized troops dispatched to Egypt from Britain in the summer of 1940 while a German invasion was still probable. The Chief of Staff and the War Cabinet accepted a risk, and events have abundantly justified them in taking it. The army under General Wavell's command was also reinforced from many other quarters, but in the Libyan campaign the chief part was played by a very small force of British armoured and mechanized troops and Australian infantry carried in lorries. Small groups of the Free French cooperated in the extreme South from French Equatorial Africa.

The British forestalled a carefully prepared Italian invasion of Egypt by a few days and in swift succession captured one heavily fortified Italian coastal stronghold after another, taking over a hundred and eighty thousand prisoners, inflicting heavy casualties, and capturing very large stocks of war material at the cost of a few hundred British casualties.

The campaign would have been impossible without the full cooperation of the British navy and the Royal Air Force. For this reason the Libyan campaign will forever remain a model of combined operations on land, on sea, and in the air. The navy protected the army's right flank and provided the troops with water and stores which were landed along the Libyan coast. After the capture of Bardia the navy assisted by transporting to Egypt many thousands of prisoners whose presence hampered the British advance. Other ships of the navy bombarded Italian fortified positions prior to attacks on them from the land.

An equally essential part was played by the Royal Air Force. It was necessary to obtain complete mastery of the air, to drive the Italians right out of the sky, and, in particular, to prevent reconnaissance. This was carried out so effectively that towards the end of the campaign the Italians were completely in the dark as to the movements of British armoured and motorized columns driving over the open desert. There was no cover or possibility of concealment for our troops, yet from the initial attack until the end of the campaign they achieved one surprise after another. In the end they made a forced march over very bad country inland of the coastal range and placed themselves astride the road along which the Italian army was retreating from Benghazi. Such operations would have been impossible without British mastery of the air.

It was secured by persistent bombing of Italian aerodromes, the destruction of large numbers of enemy aircraft on the ground, and by British superiority in air fighting. The destruction of the Italian air force and the interception of reconnaissance aircraft was thus the principal objective of the Royal Air Force. During the month of February 1941, 149 enemy aircraft were found burned out, wrecked, or abandoned on enemy aerodromes occupied by our forces. In addition to this, Italian ships, docks, munition dumps, and troops were bombed and machine-gunned from the air.

Most versatile of all was a Hurricane pilot who captured a number of prisoners. Observing a body of Italians retreating over the desert to the west, he first dived on them, firing warning bursts in front of them, and succeeded in turning them back. Whenever they attempted to break away towards the west he dived and fired again and soon had an orderly body, which he rounded up like a sheep dog, travelling towards the east. He was later able to call up British troops to take charge of his little flock. What a contrast between that incident and the German air force machine-gunning of helpless refugees on the French and Belgian roads the previous summer! A member of the Hitler Youth, proud as a German pilot to graduate in murdering old and young and innocent, and the humorous pilot of that Hurricane who refrained from killing the uniformed enemy because it was too easy are fitting representatives of their countries and the causes for which they fight.

Long before the British forces had cut off the Italian army, greatly superior to them in numbers, in its retreat from Benghazi, and the elusive General Berganzoli was "in the bag" the Royal Air Force had obtained complete mastery in the air over the Italian and the few German aircraft in Libya at that time. One reason for this was that the Italians had difficulties in the maintenance of their aircraft in Libya, owing to the shortage of spares and of supplies of all kinds. The shortage of aero engines was acute. Owing to these difficulties, it is stated that 70 per cent of the aircraft of some units of the Italian air force were unserviceable.

The shortage of supplies may have been partly due to the sinking of particular transports by British submarines. But it reflected the growing difficulties of the Italian aircraft industry owing to lack of materials and the strain of war on a country which has been on the verge of bankruptcy for many years.

The chief reason for the eclipse of the Italian air force was, however, the quality of the British fighter squadrons. Originally equipped with Gladiators, the Middle East command had been reinforced with some Hurricane squadrons which were greatly superior to anything the Italians could put up against them. Long before the Libyan campaign opened the Royal Air Force had been exacting heavy toll from the Italians and from the beginning had established an ascendancy over the Italian pilots.

Thus on August 8, 1940, thirteen Gladiators attacked twenty-seven Italian fighters and shot down fifteen of them. We lost two aircraft, but one of the pilots was saved.

The figures for the eight weeks of August and September 1940 show that our Gladiators had almost exactly the same ascendancy over the Italian aircraft as the Hurricanes and Spitfires at home had over the Germans. Thirty-five British aircraft were lost in these eight weeks against one hundred and forty-five Italian aircraft shot down. These are the confirmed Italian losses, excluding the "probables" and the severely damaged aircraft. The ratio is rather better than four to one.

By the time the Hurricane squadrons arrived and before the Libyan campaign opened the process of attrition had been going on some time. British mastery of the air, the persistent success of the British navy in taking convoys through the Mediterranean, and the failure of Italian air attacks on Malta led the Axis partners to transfer a large force of German fighters and dive bombers to the south of Italy, where they could attack the British fleet, British convoys, and Malta. A few German aircraft were transferred to Libyan air bases. It was not, however, until after the campaign that German aircraft were transferred in large numbers to Tripolitania and, after the recapture of Libya, to the Libyan air bases.

The delay in sending the German air force to Libya appears to be one more example of the fact which is so paradoxical and so imperfectly understood: *that aircraft are one of the least mobile arms.* Aircraft can only operate efficiently from well-equipped bases, and the establishment and organization of such bases takes time.

After the capture of Benghazi the British army paused for several weeks, making no attempt to follow up its extraordinary success further by the capture of Tripolitania, the chief towns of which were separated from it by four hundred miles of almost waterless desert. The decision to halt was no doubt due to the need to refit and overhaul the tanks and lorries of the small forces which had been employed and to rest the troops who had been fighting for many weeks, often in sandstorms, and living under the most difficult and exhausting conditions.

At all events, it was decided to launch a campaign for the conquest of Abyssinia and the restoration of the Emperor Haile Selassie. The Abyssinian campaign has been triumphantly carried out, and only a few hundred Italians are still holding out. The Duke of Aosta has surrendered at the time of writing.

The halt in our campaign in Libya must be regretted. Had the British forces pushed on to the capture of Tripolitania they would have established contact with French territory, and the results might have been far reaching.

Meanwhile a new complication, involving British honour and the good name of Britain throughout the Middle East, was developing in the Balkans and was to lead to a short campaign in Greece.

Early in 1941 Germany began to occupy Bulgaria, beginning with the construction and equipment of numerous bases for her air force. When these were completed German troops occupied Bulgaria, and German diplomacy began to exert its familiar blackmail on

Jugoslavia. The signing of the Tripartite Pact by the Jugoslav government was followed by a *coup d'état* in which King Peter assumed power and the regent, Prince Paul, left the country. Before the new Jugoslav government could redistribute the Jugoslav army the German forces in Bulgaria struck in the south of Jugoslavia.

Mr. Eden, the British Foreign Secretary, and Sir John Dill, Chief of the Imperial General Staff, visited Greece and Turkey and Egypt in March 1941. The Greek government had informed them that whether they received help from Britain or not they would resist the impending attack by Germany. Britain had guaranteed Greek independence before the outbreak of war just as she had guaranteed that of Poland.

It was in these circumstances and with the concurrence of General Wavell that the British War Cabinet decided to send an expeditionary force to Greece.

The transport of this force from Egypt was entrusted to the navy, and while it was still in progress, about midday on March 27, reconnaissance by aircraft of the Royal Air Force showed that enemy cruisers were steaming east of Cape Passero in the extreme south of Sicily. Three battleships, twelve cruisers, and fourteen destroyers are later reported to have composed this force which was therefore practically the entire Italian navy. Admiral Cunningham was at Alexandria with his main forces, and in the words of the naval communiqué: "It was immediately clear to him that these enemy cruisers could not be up to any good." He concluded their intention was to attack our convoys between Egypt and Greece.

He at once dispatched his light forces, consisting of H.M.S. *Orion* with the cruisers *Ajax*, *Perth*, and *Gloucester* and some destroyers, to a position south of Crete. He himself, with the battleships *Warspite*, *Valiant*, and *Barham*, the aircraft carrier *Formidable*, and some destroyers, steamed to the northwest of Alexandria.

Meanwhile a big air attack was launched on the aerodrome at Lecce in southern Italy. This was in order to put out of action as many of the German dive bombers stationed there as possible. For it might be that a secondary object of the Italian fleet, if they met British naval forces, was to lure them within striking distance of the German dive bombers. In that case the Italian fleet would be the bait, and the Stukas the trap. The attack on Lecce seems to have been planned to spring the trap.

At seven forty-nine on Friday morning air reconnaissance reported an Italian fleet consisting of one Littorio-class (35,000 tons) battleship with six cruisers and seven destroyers steaming to the southeast. Soon after being sighted it was joined by two more cruisers and at least two more destroyers. The British light forces were about forty miles to the southeast of the Italians. The main fleet with Admiral Cunningham was about ninety-five miles farther to the southeast and was steaming northwest. On making contact with the enemy our cruiser force turned and steamed southeast to draw the enemy towards our approaching battleships.

About 9 A.M. the Italian force turned about and began steaming northwest. The British cruiser force followed suit. About eleven they found themselves pressing too closely on the Littorio-class battleship and turned southeast to keep out of range of her heavy guns. The Italians followed them. At half-past eleven a torpedo attack was launched on the Littorio-class battleship by aircraft from the aircraft carrier *Formidable*. One possible hit was claimed from this attack. The Littorio-class battleship and her cruisers turned once more to the northwest and headed for her base. After this the British cruiser force lost touch with the Littorio-class battleship, which was not afterwards sighted by our surface craft.

Meanwhile our reconnaissance aircraft had reported another enemy force consisting of two Cavour-class battleships, three cruisers, and four destroyers. Another torpedo attack was made on the Littorio-class battleship, and once more one hit was claimed on her.

In the early hours of the afternoon the Littorio-class battleship was again found by naval aircraft, and a third attack was made in which three torpedo hits were claimed.

Admiral Cunningham had meanwhile requested the cooperation of the Royal Air Force. Two squadrons of Blenheim bombers were fortunately available at an aerodrome in Crete and were immediately dispatched to attack the Italian fleet and to delay it until the slower British ships could come up with it.

Between 3 and 5 P.M. the Royal Air Force bombers attacked the Cavour-class battleships and their attendant force. In these attacks two direct hits were scored on one cruiser, one direct hit on a destroyer, and two probable hits on another cruiser. In order to delay the Italian ships still further our aircraft continued to make dives on them when they had no more bombs left so as to force them to take avoiding action.

At dusk two further torpedo attacks were made by naval aircraft. It is not thought that the Littorio-class battleship was hit, but one enemy cruiser was definitely hit by a torpedo. The British light forces regained touch with the enemy after dusk, and British destroyers were ordered to attack. At 10:10 P.M. a damaged enemy cruiser was reported three miles to port of the British battle fleet. This was the Italian cruiser *Pola*. While the British battleships approached the *Pola* they sighted three enemy cruisers crossing their bows. The leading cruiser was illuminated by searchlights from the British

destroyer *Greyhound,* and the British battleships opened fire with their fifteen-inch guns at a range of four
thousand yards. Both the Zara-class cruisers were
knocked out, as far as fighting was concerned.

Italian destroyers accompanying the cruisers were
seen to turn and fire torpedoes, and the British battleships turned to avoid them. What followed in the darkness is obscure. It is known that two of the British destroyers did considerable execution, finishing off the
three cruisers *Pola, Zara,* and *Fiume.*

Besides these three heavy cruisers, a light cruiser of
the Colleone class was probably sunk. The large Italian
destroyer *Vincenzo Gioberti* was sunk, and the destroyer *Maestrale* was sunk. The large destroyer *Alfieri*
was probably sunk. The Littorio-class battleship is believed to have escaped in the darkness but must certainly have suffered underwater damage. It is believed
that during the night she became heavily engaged with
her own forces, as during the night heavy gunfire was
heard at a time when no British forces were engaged.
Let us hope her gunnery was more accurate than it had
been earlier in the day.

No British ship sustained damage or casualties. The
total British naval losses were two aircraft of the Fleet
Air Arm. In addition we lost one Blenheim bomber of
the Royal Air Force. The Admiralty claim the battle
of Matapan was historic in two respects.

"It is the first occasion in history in which skillful co-ordination of naval operations with attacks launched by aircraft have resulted in the enemy's speed being reduced and our main units being able to force action upon a reluctant enemy. It is also the first occasion in naval history in which such severe losses have been imposed upon the enemy while our own forces were completely unscathed."

The following day British ships were engaged in rescuing Italian survivors when an attack was made upon them by German dive bombers. One Ju. 88 was shot down, and Admiral Cunningham ordered the abandonment of the rescue operations in order not to expose his ships and the Italian survivors to further dive-bombing attacks. He thereupon sent a wireless signal to the Chief of the Italian Naval Staff stating that about three hundred and fifty Italian seamen were floating on rafts and giving their position and stating that a fast hospital ship should be dispatched. Fifty-five Italian officers and eight hundred and fifty men had been picked up before British rescue work had to be abandoned. They included Captain Despini of the *Pola*. Admiral Cantoni on the *Zara* is believed to have perished.

The commander in chief of the Italian navy sent a signal thanking Admiral Cunningham for his message and stating that the hospital ship *Gradisca* had been dispatched from Taranto the previous day at 5 P.M.

The entire action shows once more that Admiral Cunningham is a sailor who understands the value of air power and how to employ it in collaboration with the fleet.

Let us for a moment look at the operations in the Middle East, from the point of view of the Germans, just a year after their victorious occupation of Denmark and conquest of Norway.

They had occupied Rumania and Bulgaria without resistance and had prepared numerous air bases in the latter country from which they could maintain complete mastery in the air over Jugoslavia, Greece, and Turkey, should the latter country become involved. When the Jugoslav *coup d'état* occurred Jugoslavia was not in a position to resist. Her army was not mechanized; her air force was negligible, and her troops were not completely mobilized. All the old military arithmetic estimating the strength of countries in terms of bayonets is out of date and meaningless. It made no difference whether Jugoslavia had half a million or three quarters of a million or a million men under arms. She had no air force and she could not stand up to air bombardment and German tanks.

Since Jugoslavia and Greece had no common plan and the small Greek army was concentrated either in Albania or on the Bulgarian frontier, the German plan was to drive through the south of Jugoslavia and thence into Greece. This would turn the Greek and British line and probably trap the greater part of the Greek army in Albania which would be forced to surrender.

When in March it became clear that not only would the Greeks fight but that the British were depleting their small forces in Libya and Egypt in order to come to their assistance it seemed to the German commanders that not only could Jugoslavia be overrun and Greece conquered but that Libya could be recaptured and Egypt immediately threatened. So it fell out.

While the British navy was engaged in escorting and protecting convoys carrying nearly sixty thousand British troops to Greece and the Royal Air Force was establishing itself in aerodromes near Athens and Larissa enemy transports loaded with German tanks and munitions crossed by night from Italy to Tripolitania or even further west to the Vichy-controlled French colony of Tunisia without being detected or attacked by the British.

Meanwhile troop-carrying Ju. 52 aircraft brought personnel and after the initial success had driven the British small forces out of Libya supplied the German and Italian forces with food, water, fuel, and ammunition in the desert.

The attack on Greece, launched on April 6, went according to plan. An attack across the Bulgarian frontier, down the river Struma, was held by the Greeks with the greatest gallantry in spite of very heavy air attack and the employment of parachute troops. A few miles to the north the Germans drove with little opposition up the Strumitza into Jugoslavia. From there the armoured divisions drove with great speed and success down the Vardar Valley to capture Salonika. Further north two armoured and one motorized division passed through the Monastir Gap and entered Greece north of Florina.

British bomber aircraft, as in France, were employed in delaying the enemy advance. Unfortunately five days of very bad weather with low cloud came at the critical time. It was during this that the German forces were able to pass through the Monastir Gap.

Just as the Germans turned the Maginot Line by their attack through Luxemburg and Belgium, in Greece they turned the position taken up by the British and Greeks. Our line depended upon Jugoslavia either remaining a firm neutral or holding the southern passes on the Bulgarian frontier. This the Jugoslavs were unable to do, and the German armoured divisions, racing through them, were able to strike south from Monastir and capture Florina. During this they were opposed at first only by the hastily assembled Mackay Force and by Greek frontier guards. The only Greek cavalry division then held them north of Florina and fought magnificently. It must have been practically annihilated, but it helped to give time for the British and Greek line to fall back, first to the line of the Peneios River and afterwards to Thermopylae.

Florina was the railhead for supplies to the Greek army in Albania, and the principal road for supplying that army was cut when the Germans reached Florina.

The Adolf Hitler S.S. motorized division turned west and before reaching Kalabaka crossed the Pindus Mountains, captured Yannina, and thereby completely cut off the main Greek army which was still in Albania.

Meanwhile three German armoured divisions had attacked the British force of two infantry divisions, one Australian and one New Zealand, and an armoured brigade. In addition a German mountain division (infantry) came down the coast from Mount Olympus to Volos, part of it afterwards crossing to the island of Euboea.

The German forces outnumbered the British in tanks by rather more than ten to one, while their air superiority towards the end of the campaign was almost absolute.

As the British fell back their advanced air bases on the Larissa plain became untenable. British fighters were then limited to the aerodrome at Athens and a smaller one at Argos, both of which were almost continuously attacked from the air. In the closing stages of the campaign British fighters could do practically nothing to interfere with German air attacks on our troops. They were almost continuously engaged in defending themselves against greatly superior odds. Thus in Greece the position we had enjoyed against the Italians in Libya was reversed.

A feature of the German advance was the swiftness with which the German air force occupied aerodromes just behind their advancing troops and operated from them.

In spite of the enemy's superiority in tanks and mechanized arms of all kinds and of his almost complete command of the air the British and Dominion troops fought back magnificently. The German losses on the Peneios gorge, at Servia, and south of Lamia at Thermopylae were very great, and the total German losses very greatly exceeded the three thousand British casualties.

Incidentally, the parallel of Leonidas and his three hundred Spartans holding the Persians at Thermopylae must not be pushed too closely, for Thermopylae itself has altered almost as much as man's weapons during the 2421 years which have elapsed. In the time of Leonidas the pass was a defile about fourteen yards wide. Since then there has been silting up of the valley, and the pass is now several miles across.

Though the Royal Air Force could do little to interfere with German bombing attacks upon our troops in the closing stages of the Greek campaign it played a considerable part in assisting the evacuation.

King Peter of Jugoslavia and members of his government were rescued from Jugoslavia. And a proportion of the British forces in Greece were brought off by our Sunderlands, by British civil flying boats of the Overseas Airways Corporation, by our bombers, and even by captured enemy aircraft. On one trip a Sunderland managed to bring off eighty-five persons including the crew of the aircraft. The normal maximum is twenty-five or thirty. The evacuation had to be carried out by night from open beaches and small ports. Pilots were therefore called upon to fly at night and alight in creeks and inlets at points unknown to them on the Greek coast. These Sunderland crews were carrying out reconnaissance in the Mediterranean throughout the daylight hours. They were flying nearly twenty-four hours a day for several days.

Owing to the lack of adequate fighter protection, the daylight embarkation of troops was too hazardous. Unlike Dunkirk, everything had to be done at night, while the troops kept, as far as possible, under cover during the day.

Besides preventing evacuation during daylight, the German air force took a large part in the closing stages of the campaign. Parachutists were dropped in large numbers near Corinth and these joined up later with the troops of the S.S. Adolf Hitler division who had struck south after reaching Yannina and had crossed to the Peloponnese at Patras. It was this force which finally brought the evacuation of forces from the neighbourhood of Nauplia to an end.

Moreover, the advance of the German mechanized forces, in spite of their ten-to-one superiority in tanks, would have been impossible without superiority in the air. Just as in France, the tanks were continually forced to a halt and then "whistled up their air." The dependance of German mechanized troops on air support is a matter of immense importance, since it looks as though the British would obtain air superiority long before they can hope to obtain superiority in armoured vehicles. Moreover, aircraft can fly the Atlantic; tanks must be shipped.

The German air force during the evacuation made most of the Greek major ports unusable. Three empty transports were sunk by bombing attacks, and after troops had been withdrawn from Nauplia by night a transport was bombed and set on fire while heavily laden. Next morning two British destroyers which had stood by the burning transport and had picked up survivors from it were sunk by repeated bombing attacks. Survivors in the water were repeatedly machine-gunned.

The German air force can also credit itself with the

sinking of most of the Greek hospital ships, clearly marked with the Red Cross, whose presence had been notified to the German authorities.

The chief glory of the short Greek campaign lies, not with the troops who fought back so stoutly and who inflicted disproportionate losses on the enemy, nor with the inadequate contingent of the Royal Air Force, but with the navy. While covering the convoys taking the troops to Greece the navy won a historic victory over the Italian fleet and the navy carried out the evacuation with extraordinary efficiency under supremely difficult circumstances.

The evacuation of Greece left the Middle East command facing an entirely new position. At the time of writing the Abyssinian campaign has drawn to a victorious close; the German advance on Egypt from Libya has been halted; Tobruk is being held, and the rebellion in Irak has been crushed. But German bombers are within easy reach of the Suez Canal, and the difficulties facing the commander in chief are immense. Not the least of them is that Britain is unable at present to achieve superiority in the air.

During April, however, eighty-one enemy aircraft were shot down by our fighters in the Western desert; eleven were destroyed by anti-aircraft fire, and thirty-one were destroyed on the ground.

In the whole of the Middle East command, including

operations in Greece as well as Abyssinia and East Africa, British losses were fifty-eight aircraft during April as against two hundred and fifty-two enemy aircraft destroyed.

Two criticisms of operations in the Middle East are frequently heard. The first is that we should not have gone to the help of Greece. The second is that we should not have launched a campaign in Abyssinia but have continued our drive from Libya to Tripoli. The first of these criticisms ignores political and moral considerations of importance. It was a matter of honour to help Greece, and although we could not do much we made the Germans suffer very heavy losses and avoided anything in the nature of a disaster to ourselves.

The second criticism reveals ignorance of the realities of the situation. The forces launched in converging columns on Abyssinia could not have been profitably diverted to a campaign against Tripoli. They consisted of Indian troops and infantry who could not have been maintained in the desert. Moreover, the drive against Abyssinia had already begun with successful operations by West, East, and South African forces operating from Kenya and the Sudan and with the cooperation of the South African and Rhodesian air forces. These could not have been diverted to Libya while the Italians maintained an air force in East Africa and Abyssinia. Nor would Abyssinian patriot activities have been possible outside their country. Had they failed to receive support the Abyssinian patriots would quite possibly have been crushed, and a rising would not necessarily have occurred later.

General Wavell must not be blamed for having achieved a victorious campaign and for having restored the Emperor Haile Selassie to his throne.

CHAPTER XVI

Help from the United States

THE FOREGOING CHAPTERS should have made it clear that the present war is being waged with three principal weapons: tanks, submarines, and aircraft. Both the tank on land and the submarine under the sea depend for their successful employment on the assistance of aircraft, and it is aircraft that are the most potent weapons in their destruction. It was mastery of the air which enabled the Germans to win their victories in Norway, Holland, Belgium, and France and in Jugoslavia and Greece. Mastery of the air won the battle of Britain for us, and we may hope that mastery of the air may decide the battle of the Atlantic in our favour.

General Wavell's victories over the Italian armies in Libya and Abyssinia would have been impossible without local superiority in the air. The two great naval victories of the war, Taranto and Matapan, were won in the first case by aircraft acting alone, in the second by the cooperation of air and sea power. It is therefore fairly obvious that the war will be won, not on land and not on or under the sea, but in the air. By this I do not for a moment mean by the exclusive use of air power. Rather, I would say that until Britain obtains unquestioned mastery of the air she cannot win.

Nor, for that matter, can she lose until Germany can obtain complete mastery in the air over Britain or over the Atlantic approaches. The duration of the war will therefore depend upon the time necessary before Britain can build up an air force very much more powerful than that of Germany. Without American help I believe that this would prove either impossible or at best an extremely slow business. Fortunately help from the United States is now assured, and the flow of American-built aircraft to this country is rapidly increasing, though it will have to be very much greater than at present if we are to hope for an early decision.

Perhaps this is a place in which I may give a guess at the way in which victory will finally be achieved. I believe that, just as the last war was won principally by the blockade by sea which lowered German standards of living, the present war will be won by the combined effects of the blockade by sea and the strategic offensive from the air. As I have already pointed out, such an offensive directed against German industry partakes of the nature of an extension of the blockade. More and more Germany's war effort will be directed to keeping the wheels turning. As the strain of continuous air attack without respite and on the heaviest possible scale grows greater German domination of the subject races of Europe will crack.

It is then that national risings, armed and instigated by the patriots serving with the British and cooperating with British armoured forces, will break out in the form of a series of guerrilla campaigns. We must expect the first few of these to be defeated, then suddenly the German war machine will break, and the tide of victory will sweep over Europe.

It is very likely that such military campaigns will apparently win us victory and that the pressure of our blockade by sea and our strategic offensive in the air which have made such operations possible will seem less important. But victory, nevertheless, will have been due to them. Nor will such military operations as may apparently end the war be possible without air cooperation and mastery of the air.

To win the war, therefore, we want, above all things, aircraft and then more aircraft. And especially we want *heavy bombers* which can carry very heavy loads to the furthest corners in which Germany may establish her factories.

A few days ago I had the privilege of visiting one of the many widely dispersed centres where American-built aircraft are received. Until this spring a large proportion of such aircraft had been originally ordered by the French and had been built to their specifications. This fact has involved their complete re-equipment, for it is hardly necessary to point out that it is essential that all equipment should be standard. Otherwise an aircraft, or many aircraft, may be grounded, owing to some minor defect and the absence of spare parts of non-standard pattern.

Moreover, these aircraft, built for France, needed more powerful armament and protective armour today. There was therefore a lot to be done to them. In widely dispersed localities I saw all the processes involved in the re-equipment of the Douglas D.B. 7, which is now coming through in large numbers. When specially armed and equipped the D.B. 7 becomes the Havoc, which is the latest type of night fighter.

I watched every stage from the unpacking of crates stencilled with the words, "French Order," to the testing of engines and the installation of a heavy armament. In the aggregate hundreds of ex-garage mechanics were busy on these skilled jobs while thousands of girls from mill and factory were busy with the less skilled or unskilled jobs.

In another place, "somewhere in Britain," I saw the

D.B. 7 going through its paces in the air. It is a magnificent aircraft, very fast and manoeuvrable, and I was particularly interested in the technique of landing an aircraft with a tricycle undercarriage. The tail of the D.B. 7 is upswept like that of a flying boat, and at first glance it may be taken for a flying boat in the air. Just as the tail of a flying boat is carried high to be out of the way of a breaking sea, so the tail of the D.B. 7 is built high to avoid its coming in contact with the ground. The fuselage is horizontal with the ground on landing.

It is a perfectly proportioned aircraft with a slim fuselage and tapered wings. It is exactly what is wanted, not only as a night fighter, but as a medium bomber for Coastal Command. Directly the United States manufacturers can equip the aircraft they are building so that they can go straight into service on arrival an enormous saving of time will be effected. There must be no time lag between the lessons learned in actual fighting and the production schedules in the United States. It is madness to go on producing aircraft ordered for operational work which need either to be adapted for it or which have to serve as trainers, since they are not up to modern operational requirements.

I believe that Britain's weakness today is greatest in bombers and particularly in heavy bombers. It is therefore in the production of heavy bombers, such as the Boeing Flying Fortress, that the United States can make its greatest contribution to winning the war. These aircraft are flown over so that there is no question of their being sunk by German submarines on the way. I had the pleasure of closely examining a Flying Fortress. We need two or three thousand such aircraft. When we have a striking force of that number of heavy bombers and a sufficient flow of production to maintain it the war will be won.

United States help will take many other forms. There is no reason why the American aircraft industry should not manufacture British types where these have proved themselves. In particular it is to be hoped that the Halford Napier Sabre engine, which, by all accounts, is by far the finest aircraft engine in the world, will be manufactured in the United States.

In engine assembly and repair sheds I have seen the splendid Allison liquid-cooled engine, built in the United States. This is the power unit for the Tomahawk fighter, which makes it greatly superior to the earlier Mohawk, fitted with the Wright Cyclone air-cooled engine.

The present trend of political events has brought the United States of America to the verge of war. It is therefore important to consider what benefits would accrue to the cause of the democracies from actual American participation in the war. The naval help resulting from such an entry would be immense, and the battle of the Atlantic would be won. But it is of vital importance that if the United States does participate directly the mistakes which attended her entry into the last war should be avoided. We must, at all costs, learn the lessons of recent history which thousands of us can remember. These lessons are recorded in the pages of the official histories of the last war. The following passages should be kept in mind by all responsible citizens of the United States, by journalists and broadcasters as well as by politicians and the military, naval, and air advisers of that country.

"The story of the intervention of America in the war contains some lessons of interest. . . . So far as concerns supply, it may be said that America was on the side of the Allies from the beginning. When, however, she began to organize forces of her own, subsequent to her declaration of war, she could do so only at the expense of the Allies in the early stages, even though great general benefits would ultimately accrue from American intervention on a national scale. What America did, in effect, was to step into all markets equipped with absolute priorities."[1]

Mr. Jones, the official historian, traces in other pages

[1] *The War in the Air*, Vol. VI, p. 80.

the disastrous effect upon the expansion and equipment of the Royal Air Force resulting from United States intervention.

Mr. Ryan, U.S. Undersecretary for Aviation, informed Mr. Churchill in September 1918 that the American Admiralty claimed absolute priority for the Liberty engine. And Mr. Churchill[2] reported in a memorandum that "a great part of these precious engines on which the whole of our air-offensive bombing program depends has, up to date, been swallowed up by American aviation." In fact, only a handful of the many thousands of Liberty engines contracted for or built ever played any part in the war. What was true of engines was true of silver spruce of which aircraft were then built. British pilots had to fly over the front line and engage in combat with Goering's famous squadron in aircraft built of wood below specification and with engines below specification in order that pilots might be trained in the United States. The war was over before their training was completed.

It is clear that the same causes will lead to the same results if the United States enters the war today unless these lessons have been learned and are constantly borne in mind. The difficulty then was undoubtedly that the necessity of completely separate national services was taken for granted. Anything else would have wounded

[2] *Ibid.*, Vol. VI, p. 53.

national pride. Today the British Air Force has Polish, Czech, Free French, and probably Greek squadrons attached to it as well as contingents from Canada, South Africa, New Zealand, and Australia, working easily within its framework.

If the United States enters this war, is it too much to hope that it will cooperate in the same way? That it will send a contingent which, beginning perhaps with a few squadrons, would grow as vast as circumstances may require but which would work, not under British direction, but within the same framework? We are fighting for freedom today—not for the predominance of certain labels or the prestige of uniforms and corps.

If it be the will of the American people to enter the war let them see to it that the flow of aircraft to Britain is not held up, whether they come with trained crews to fight them or without. My own belief is that the United States can play the decisive part in the war without formal participation in it. The more pilots who come to take a hand, like those of the Eagle Squadron, or in units under their United States commanding officers, the better. There is plenty of work for all.

APPENDIX

Operational Aircraft of the Royal Air Force and the German Air Force

---

THE ROYAL AIR FORCE

SINGLE-ENGINED FIGHTERS

The only biplane fighter in the Royal Air Force with which we need concern ourselves is the Gloster Gladiator. Being a biplane, it is obsolete on account of its lack of speed but in all other respects it is first rate. It was the best fighter in the world until the monoplanes came along. It is extraordinarily manoeuvrable, and in the hands of highly trained aerobatic pilots the Gladiator, as we shall see, has achieved miracles in the present war. It has, however, played its part and is unlikely to be heard of very much in the future. In one respect, however, the Gladiator has important practical advantages over the monoplanes which have superseded it.

It can take off and land on smaller and rougher airfields under worse conditions. The use of aircraft with retractable undercarriages in snow often gives trouble. Gladiators were thus very useful in Norway and Finland.

The Gladiator has staggered wings of 32-foot span, a Bristol radial air-cooled Mercury engine and a top speed of 250 m.p.h. It is armed with four or six machine guns.

The Hawker Hurricane is a single-seater low-wing monoplane with wings of 40-foot span. It has a Rolls-Royce Merlin 1030 h.p. engine which gives a top speed of 335 m.p.h. It has a retractable undercarriage. It is armed with eight Browning machine guns, four in either wing, arranged to fire outside the disc of the three-bladed airscrew which is of variable pitch.

The Hurricane has had two advantages over the German fighters it has come up against in the first eighteen months of the war. It is more manoeuvrable and it is more heavily armed. The pilot is also protected by armour, back and front. To some extent the Hurricane shares the advantage of being able to operate from small fields and in rough country. It has been flown from aircraft carriers and can land on their decks, and the undercarriage, being wider, enables safe landings to be made where a Spitfire would turn over. The initial climb, 2400 feet per minute, is slightly higher than that of the Spitfire.

The Spitfire, however, is definitely better in performance than the Hurricane. It is a single-seater, all-metal, low-wing monoplane with elliptical wings and a very carefully stream-lined fuselage. The wings have a span of 36 feet, 10 inches. It is said that there is not a straight line anywhere on the skin of a Spitfire. The armament, armour, and engine of the Spitfire are normally the same as those of the Hurricane; the latter gives it a top speed of 366 m.p.h. The initial climb is 2300 feet per minute.

Like all superlatively good aircraft, the Spitfire looks right to the eye, but its beauty depends not only on the perfection of the streamlining but on the elliptical wings.

The Boulton Paul Defiant is a freak fighter in that it is a small two-seater. The disadvantage of most single-seater fighters is that the armament consists of fixed guns, and the pilot can only attack an enemy when he is heading for him. A two-seater fighter can attack when it is flying on a course parallel with that of the enemy and from all sorts of angles. The enemy who is only expecting a single-seater fighter can easily be taken at a disadvantage by such an aircraft as the Defiant. On the other hand, it is impossible that two men, however practised, should be able to achieve the lightning decision of one. For this reason I believe that unless it becomes possible for fighting to be carried out in close formation by large numbers of aircraft the two-seater fighter will always be at a disadvantage in a dogfight with a single-seater fighter during daylight.

The Defiant has been used as a night fighter. The Defiant is an all-metal low-wing monoplane armed with four Browning machine guns mounted in a power-operated turret behind the pilot. It has a Merlin Rolls-Royce 1030 h.p. engine. The wing span is 39 feet 6 inches.

The Tornado was not heard of by the British public until 1941. It is, as its name indicates, a super Hurricane, but no details are available as to its performance.

The Typhoon—The existence of the Typhoon was made known during April 1941 and was splashed in the newspapers shortly before Lord Beaverbrook relinquished the office of Minister of Aircraft Production. The Typhoon is a very small aircraft, designed by Mr. Sydney Camm, and has been built round the new Halford Napier Sabre liquid-cooled engine which those who know assert is the finest aircraft engine in the world. The Typhoon is armed with cannon and machine guns, is heavily armoured, and has a top speed considerably in excess of any fighter aircraft in the world.

The following American single-seater fighters are in service with the Royal Air Force or the Fleet Air Arm:

Buffalo 1 (Brewster 339)

A midwing monoplane with retractable undercarriage. Span, 35 feet, length, 26 feet, wing area, 208.9 sq. feet. The Buffalo has a Wright GR.1830 G.205A engine and a speed of 310 m.p.h.

Martlet 1 (Grumman G.36A)

A midwing monoplane with an undercarriage which retracts sideways into the fuselage, a single-seater with fixed wings. Span, 38 feet, length, 28 feet 5 inches. Same engine as the Buffalo.

Mohawk 1 (Curtiss Hawk 75a-4)

A single-seater low-wing monoplane with an undercarriage, rotating through 90° and folding backwards. Span, 37 feet 3½ inches, length, 28 feet 9½ inches. It has the Wright GR.1820 G.205 air-cooled engine.

Tomahawk 1 (Curtiss Hawk 81)

A single-seater low-wing monoplane. The undercarriage retracts backwards, rotating through 90° as in the earlier Curtiss Hawk 75a. Span, 37 feet 3½ inches, length, 28 feet 11 inches.

The Tomahawk has an Allison V1710-C15 liquid-cooled engine. It is the best of the bunch listed above and is credited with a speed of about 400 m.p.h. The Tomahawk is in operational use in Britain and can often be seen overhead.

TWIN-ENGINED FIGHTERS

The only twin-engined fighters with which we need concern ourselves are the Bristol Blenheim, which is also used as a reconnaissance aircraft and as a medium bomber, and the improved version of the Blenheim which in its fighter form is known as the Bristol Beaufighter and the Douglas D.B.7.

The Blenheim is one of the first monoplanes with which the Royal Air Force was equipped and has been several years in service. It has proved itself an aircraft of many virtues. It is an all-round aircraft and has given admirable service with Bomber, Coastal, and Fighter Commands under all sorts of conditions and has proved its worth from Finland to Greece.

Two Bristol 930 h.p. Mercury XV engines give a speed of 285 m.p.h. It has tapered wings of 56 feet, 4 inches span. It carries a crew of three and has a range of 2000 miles. There is a power-operated gun turret on the top of the fuselage. As a fighter the Blenheim is armed with four machine guns under the nose as well as one in the turret. The bomber has only the turret guns.

The original Mark I Blenheim has been superseded by the Mark IV, which has a redesigned nose which is longer and curiously asymmetric. The retractable landing wheels are set well apart under the engine nacelles.

The Bristol Beaufighter is the fighter version of the Bristol Beaufort.

The Havoc is the Douglas D.B.7 with special armament and equipment to enable it to be used as a night fighter. The D.B.7 is a midwing twin-engined monoplane with an upturned tail, like a flying boat, and a tricycle undercarriage which retracts into the engine nacelles and the nose. There are two Pratt and Whitney air-cooled engines. The D.B.7 is a fast and extremely manoeuvrable aircraft and as a night fighter has scored many victories over German raiders both over Britain and when they were taking off or landing at their bases in northern France.

Details of the equipment and armament of the Havoc are secret.

ARMY COOPERATION

The Westland Lysander is a high-wing monoplane of peculiar appearance, owing to several distinctive features. The wings taper towards their roots as well as more sharply towards the tips. There are V bracing struts connecting the broadest part of the wing to the roots of the undercarriage legs. There are large wheel spats in which the machine guns are concealed and lateral structures from the tops of the wheel spats carry bombs, etc. The undercarriage does not retract. The wings have a span of 50 feet.

The Bristol air-cooled Perseus XII engine gives a speed of 230 m.p.h. and a range of 600 miles.

The Lysander as an army cooperation machine has a high speed range, a low landing speed, and great manoeuvrability. It is peculiarly suitable for picking up messages from the ground, dropping s.a.a. or food to troops surrounded by the enemy, and also for ground-strafing and dive-bombing.

The German counterpart is the Henschel 126.

SHORT-RANGE BOMBERS

The Fairey Battle is one of the early types of monoplane adopted in the Royal Air Force and is obsolete by modern standards. The Rolls-Royce Merlin engine gives a speed of 257 m.p.h. and a range of not more than 1000 miles. It is a two-seater monoplane of 54-foot span with a slim fuselage.

It is armed with two machine guns, one in the starboard wing and the other, manually operated, in the rear gunner's cockpit. The Battle played a historic part in the battle of France, but its slow speed and insufficient armament made it a vulnerable aircraft, and its short range limits its usefulness.

Medium Bombers
The Blenheim (see Twin-engined Fighters)

The Bristol Beaufort. The Beaufort is a refined version of the Blenheim with two 1060 h.p. Taurus II engines which give it a higher speed than the Blenheims. The forward portion of the fuselage is deeper and extends back to the turret which is fared into the aft of the cabin. The wings have a span of 57 feet 10 inches. The nose is transparent.

The Beaufort is on service with Coastal Command, armed with bombs or torpedo and machine guns. It carries a crew of four—pilot, navigator, wireless operator, and rear gunner.

The Avro Anson is a low-wing monoplane with a long windowed cabin in the metal fuselage which is covered with fabric. The wings are wooden and of 56 feet 6 inches span. It has two 350 h.p. air-cooled Armstrong Siddeley Cheetah IX engines which give it a top speed of 188 m.p.h. It carries a crew of three and is armed with fixed machine guns in the nose and others in the power-operated turret behind the long cabin. The landing wheels retract into the engine nacelles.

The Anson is obsolete as an operational aircraft but is largely used for training. Nevertheless, the Anson has done much valuable work with Coastal Command. In fighting its manoeuvrability has stood it in good stead. Thus on November 8, 1939, an Anson, attacked by a Heinkel 115 seaplane, at once went into a steep turn which it continued until the Heinkel appeared in the pilot's gun sights, owing to the Heinkel not being able to turn in so small a circle. The latter began to break up under the Anson's fire and then sank in the sea. On another occasion an Anson brought down an enemy aircraft by ramming it. The British pilot was killed.

Ansons have been used chiefly for inshore coastal work and in the narrow seas but they were also frequently engaged in reconnaissance off the Dutch coast in the first year of the war.

The Lockheed Hudson is a version of the famous Lockheed Electra air liner used extensively in civil aviation in many parts of the world. It is built by the Lockheed company in California. The Hudson is a low-wing monoplane with a long, roomy fuselage, twin rudders, and narrow tapering wings of 65 feet 6 inches span. It has two 1100 h.p. Wright Cyclone engines which give it a speed of 246 m.p.h. and a range of 1700 miles. Its armament consists of machine guns in the nose and others in the power-operated turret set far back in the rear of the fuselage. It carries a heavy load of bombs. The Hudson, like all Lockheed aircraft, obtains its speed by having relatively small wings with a high wing loading. This is only possible by the liberal use of flaps to increase the speed range and to enable it to land at a reasonable speed.

In recent years wing loadings have been pushed higher and higher, since to reduce the area of the wings is the easiest way for designers to get higher speeds. But the requirements of military are greater than that of civil aircraft, and for service purposes the Hudson suffers from lack of manoeuvrability and from its high landing speed. It carries a crew of four. If the vice of the Hudson is that it cannot be thrown about in the air, its virtues are that it is exceedingly tough, and Hudsons have returned safely after taking an extraordinary amount of punishment from enemy fighters or anti-aircraft. Another feature of the Hudson which adds to the happiness of those aboard is the air conditioning, an even and pleasant temperature being maintained by the air entering being heated by the engines. This refinement adds greatly to the efficiency of the crew when flying through snow showers along the Norwegian coast close to the Arctic Circle. Hudsons are in service with Coastal Command.

The Douglas Boston II (D.B. 7) is a twin-engined mid-wing monoplane with underslung engines built by the Douglas Aircraft Company in the U.S.A. It has a tricycle undercarriage; the outer wheels retract into the engine nacelles, and the front retracts into the fuselage.

It carries a crew of three, has a wing spread of 61 feet 4 inches and a length of 47 feet 7 inches. There are two piece trailing edge flaps to extend the speed range. There are two Pratt and Whitney R.1830-S3C4G engines. Details of performance and armament are not available. The engine nacelles project beyond the trailing edge of the wing; this fact and the flying-boat tail make the D.B. 7 easily recognizable in the air.

The fighter version is the Havoc night fighter.

The Glenn Martin Maryland I (Martin 167) is a twin-engined low-wing monoplane. It has the same engines as the Boston II. The undercarriage retracts into the engine nacelles. It has a wing span of 61 feet 4 inches and a length of 46 feet 8 inches—almost the same proportions as the Boston II—but its height from the ground is only 9 feet 7 inches as compared with 15 feet 10 inches of the Boston.

Details of performance and armament are not available. The British public has received news of this addition to the Royal Air Force in action in the Middle East.

HEAVY BOMBERS

The Wellington was out and away the best bomber possessed by any belligerent at the beginning of the war. It is a magnificent aircraft and has given magnificent performance. It is a midwing monoplane of geodetic construction. That is to say, the planes of curvature of the structural members are everywhere perpendicular to the surface of the aircraft. It is all metal with a fabric covering.

Two Bristol Pegasus XVIII air-cooled 1000 h.p. engines give it a speed of 265 m.p.h. and a range of 3200 miles. The armament consists of machine guns in power-operated turrets in the nose and tail and in a third turret which is retractable under the fuselage. There is a crew of five.

The wings of 86 feet 1 inch span and the tail plane taper sharply. There is a very distinctive tall rudder.

The Stirling.

Details of the Stirling are secret. It is a giant heavy four-engined heavy bomber built by Short Brothers, who build the Sunderland flying boat. It is the biggest bomber in operational use in the world. In general lines there is a strong resemblance to the Wellington, of which it appears to be a large four-engined version. It has been used for carrying heavy loads of the new "high-power" bombs on Berlin and other targets.

Armstrong Whitworth Whitley

The Whitley is a heavy midwing bomber which first appeared at the Hendon air-force display in 1935. Since then the original Armstrong Siddeley engines have been replaced by Rolls-Royce Merlin engines of 1030 h.p. The mark V Whitley has a later mark of Merlin engine. This has increased the top speed which is over 245 m.p.h., while the operational range is in excess of 1500 miles since Whitleys have covered that distance in operational flights.

The Whitley carries a crew of five and a bomb load of 3443 lbs. and has an armament of six machine guns in front and tail turrets.

The wings have a span of 84 feet. The Whitley has a rectangular fuselage, so straight underneath that to the eye it appears to be slightly concave, and the nose and tail appear to sag, which is an optical illusion.

The Whitley is designed as a night bomber only and, so far as I know, has been employed only as such.

The Handley Page Hampden is a twin-engined midwing monoplane with two Bristol Pegasus XVIII engines which give a top speed of 265 m.p.h. It carries a crew of four. The armament consists of machine guns in the nose, beneath the fuselage to the rear, and in a rear turret above. The Hampden is a peculiar-looking aircraft with a narrow fuselage deep in front but reduced to no more than a tail boom aft of the wings. These taper sharply forwards. The Hampden has twin fins and rudders set well apart.

The narrow fuselage of the Hampden gives a superficial resemblance to a German bomber if seen in bad light and at a distance.

The Handley Page Hereford is simply a Hampden with Napier Dagger liquid-cooled engines instead of the Bristol air-cooled radial engines.

The Liberator heavy bomber is built in California by the Consolidated Aircraft Corporation. It is a high-wing monoplane with four Pratt and Whitney engines.

The wings have a span of 110 feet and the fuselage a length of 66 feet.

The Boeing Flying Fortress is a heavy bomber with four

air-cooled engines. Details of British modifications and equipment are secret.

FLYING BOATS

The short Sunderland is a very large and stoutly constructed all-metal high-wing monoplane. The wing span is 112 feet 9 inches and the length 85 feet 4 inches.

The Sunderland has four 1010 h.p. Bristol Pegasus XXII engines, giving a top speed of 210 m.p.h. and a range of 2800 miles. The Sunderland can therefore stay out for twelve hours or more at a stretch. The fuselage is spacious in the extreme and has two decks. There is a crew of seven.

The armament consists of a power-operated gun turret in the nose which is retracted when the boat is at her moorings, a power-operated turret in the stern, and two Vickers guns amidships in pillar mountings.

The Sunderland is the largest aircraft in the service of any belligerent power.

The Saro Lerwick is a twin-engined high-wing monoplane boat of all-metal construction.

The wing span is 81 feet and the length 63 feet. The Lerwick has two Bristol Hercules engines.

The armament consists of machine guns in three power-operated turrets, one in the nose which is retracted when the boat is at her moorings, one in the stern, and one amidships above.

The Consolidated PBY 5 Catalina flying boat is a high-wing monoplane with braced wings of 104-foot span. The length of the boat is 62 feet 6 inches. There are retractable wing-tip floats. The two Pratt and Whitney air-cooled engines give a top speed of 206 m.p.h. and a range of 4000 miles. Details of the armament are secret.

AIRCRAFT OF THE FLEET AIR ARM

The Blackburn Skua is a low-wing monoplane fighter and dive bomber. The Skua has a 900 h.p. Bristol Perseus engine. The wing span is 46 feet 2 inches.

The Skua carries a crew of two and is armed with five machine guns.

The fighter version of the Skua, called the Roc, has a heavier armament of machine guns, some being carried in a power-operated turret at the rear of the cabin.

The Fairey Swordfish is a biplane used for reconnaissance and torpedo carrying. The 750 h.p. Bristol Pegasus III engine gives it a top speed of 154 m.p.h. The staggered wings have a span of 45 feet 6 inches. The Swordfish carries a crew of two or three and is armed with two machine guns. The torpedo is slung externally between the legs of the undercarriage.

The latter is interchangeable, with twin floats for use from naval vessels other than aircraft carriers without a deck. The aircraft is slung overboard and takes off from the sea.

The Fairey Albacore is a biplane with wings of equal span used for torpedo carrying, dive-bombing, etc. The engine is the Bristol Taurus.

PRINCIPAL OPERATIONAL AIRCRAFT OF THE GERMAN AIR FORCE

SINGLE-ENGINED FIGHTERS

The Messerschmitt 109 is a single-seater, low-wing, all-metal monoplane. It was originally designed for an engine of lower power than the Daimler Benz 601 1500 h.p. now used. As a result its manoeuvrability is said to have suffered, and turns to the right are executed with some difficulty.

The Me. 109 has been armed in various ways: with a cannon firing through the airscrew hub, four machine guns, and two in troughs on the top of the engine cowling.

Front and back armour for the pilot was introduced during the battle of Britain in the summer of 1940. The top speed is 350 m.p.h., greater than that of the British Hurricane but less than that of the Spitfire.

The Heinkel 113 was the first used in small numbers in the later stages of the battle of Britain in the summer of 1940.

It is a low-wing all-metal monoplane with a wing span of under 31 feet and a Daimler Benz 601 engine of about 1500 h.p. It is, as might be expected, very fast indeed—about 380 m.p.h.

The wings are not only short in themselves but they are short in relation to the length of the fuselage.

The armament is a cannon firing through the hub of the airscrew and two heavy machine guns in the wing roots.

Twin-engined Fighters

The Messerschmitt 110 is a two-seater low-wing fighter bomber. The two Daimler Benz 601 engines give a top speed of 365 m.p.h. It has tapered wings and twin rudders outside the elevator.

There are two cannons firing through the airscrew hubs and four fixed machine guns in the nose, with a manually operated gun for the second member of the crew, who sits directly behind the pilot. There is back armour only.

The Me. 110 is more difficult to manoeuvre than the Me. 109 and it has fared badly in combats with British fighters.

The Me. 110 has also been used as a light bomber in high-speed daylight raids.

It is a strikingly ugly aircraft.

Junkers 87 b

A two-seater single-engined dive bomber, frequently known as the "Stuka," which is simply the German contraction for the words "dive bomber."

The Ju. 87 b is a low-wing all-metal cantilever monoplane with a "W," or "inverted gull," wing. That is to say, the centre sections, from the fuselage to the undercarriage legs, have a decided anhedral, while the outer sections of the wings have pronounced dihedral. The fixed undercarriage has spatted wheels. The 1200 h.p. Jumo 211a engine gives a top speed of 242 m.p.h. The tapered wings have square-cut tips and large flaps the full length of the trailing edge. There are also air brakes under the wings for slowing up at the end of the dive. The tail plane is braced. The span is 45 feet 3 inches and the length 35 feet 4 inches. There is a glazed two-seater cockpit. The armament is two machine guns.

One 1100 lb. bomb and four 110 lb. bombs are usually carried.

LONG-RANGE BOMBERS
Junkers 88

The Ju. 88 is a midwing cantilever monoplane with two liquid-cooled Jumo 211a engines which give it a top speed of 317 m.p.h. An unusual feature is that the radiators are in the form of radial cowlings round the forward part of the engine nacelles. The asymmetrically tapered wings are of 59-foot span. The fuselage is 461 feet 6 inches in length. There is an asymmetric gun position below the forward part of the fuselage, a short glazed nose, and a glazed cabin above. There are external bomb racks and air brakes under the wing. There is a crew of four and an armament of three machine guns.

The Heinkel 111k is a low-wing cantilever monoplane which has been produced in various versions. The mark V has two liquid 1150 h.p. Daimler Benz engines, though aircraft with Jumo 1200 h.p. engines have been brought down. The top speed is not more than 275 m.p.h. The tapered wings are of 74 feet 3 inches span, and the length of the fuselage is 54 feet 6 inches. There is a single fin and rudder. The Heinkel 111 carries a crew of four and has an armament of three machine guns, one in the nose, one in a "blister" below the fuselage, and one on top of the fuselage.

The Dornier 17 is a high-wing cantilever monoplane with wings of 59-foot span and a long, slender fuselage 55 feet 4 inches in length.

The long nose projects in front of the two engines which may be either 1050 h.p. Daimler Benz liquid-cooled engines or 1000 h.p. Bramo air-cooled engines. The top speed is about 310 m.p.h. The twin fins and rudders are mounted outside the tail plane.

The armament consists of two fixed forward-firing machine guns and two movable machine guns, one below and one above.

The Dornier 215 is a development of the Do. 17, which it closely resembles. There is a shorter nose and a deep cockpit which projects below the line of the fuselage and has a domed glazed top. The usual engines are 1150 h.p. Daimler Benz liquid-cooled 601a, giving a top speed of 312 m.p.h.

The tail is the same as in the Do. 17. The armament is three movable machine guns, one in the nose, one below, and one above.

The Junkers 52 is a three-engined low-wing monoplane with wings of 96-foot span and fuselage 62 feet in length. The three B.M.W. radial air-cooled engines give it a top speed of 189 m.p.h. It has uniformly tapered wings with considerable dihedral. The fuselage and wings are constructed of corrugated sheet metal which was typical of early Junkers construction. Flaps run the full length of the wings. There is a single fin and rudder and a long braced tail plane. The spatted undercarriage does not retract.

The Ju. 52 can carry two tons of arms and equipment for short distances or a load of fourteen parachutists with equipment. It was employed largely for the invasion of Norway and Holland and has recently been used to supply and/or reinforce German mechanized columns in Libya.

The armament consists of a machine-gun position far back on the fuselage and a machine gun in a retractable position under the fuselage.

The Junkers 86 or 86K

This low-wing twin-engined monoplane has been used by many air lines, including the South African. The civil version serves as a troop carrier, the Krieg, or K type, as a bomber.

The tapered wings have a span of 73 feet 8 inches and the fuselage a length of 57 feet 4 inches. It has twin fins and rudders set outside the braced tail plane. Flaps run the full length of the wings. The armament consists of three movable machine guns, one in the nose, one in a partly enclosed rear cockpit, and one in a retractable turret, or "dustbin," below.

Two B.M.W. air-cooled radial engines give the civil version a top speed of 233 m.p.h. The K bomber version may have either 700 h.p. Jumo Diesel engines with a top speed of 224 m.p.h. or 880 h.p. B.M.W. engines giving a top speed of 238 m.p.h.

The undercarriage retracts.

The Junkers 89 and 90

The Ju. 90 is a four-engined air liner, carrying forty passengers, which was on regular service of the Lufthansa air lines for many years. It can carry a load of seven tons.

It is a low-wing monoplane with sharply tapered wings with full dihedral of 114 feet 10 inches span. The fuselage is 86 feet 3 inches in length, with twin fins and rudders set inside the tail plane, which is not strutted and is set forward of the tail of the fuselage.

The Ju. 89 is the military version and has four 1200 h.p. Jumo liquid-cooled engines giving a top speed of about 225 m.p.h. The Ju. 90 has four 880 B.M.W. air-cooled engines and top speed of 217 m.p.h. The Ju. 89 has a glazed bombing position in the nose, a tail gun turret, and gun positions in the fuselage.

The Focke-Wulf Condor is a four-engined low-wing monoplane with a span of 108 feet 3 inches. The wings taper sharply and have rounded tips. There is a single large fin and rudder. The civil version has B.M.W. air-cooled engines and a top speed of over 230 m.p.h. The Condor is the prototype of the Kurier, which has an increased range and higher top speed and is being used to attack shipping in the Atlantic from a base near Bordeaux.

The Dornier 24 is a high-wing monoplane flying boat with braced wings tapered on the leading edge only. There are three 880 h.p. B.M.W. or Bramo Fafnir engines. The wings are of 88 feet 7 inches span and the length of the boat 72 feet. There are twin fins and rudders, and stub wings extend from the sides of the hull. There are three gun turrets, one in the nose, one amidships, and one in the tail.

The Dornier 26 is a high-wing monoplane four-engined flying boat. The "gull" wings are of 98 foot span, and their outer sections taper from the leading edge. There are retractable wing floats. The boat is 80 feet 5 inches long and has a single fin and rudder and a braced tail plane.

The four engines are fared into the wings and arranged in two pairs in tandem. During the take-off the aft engines can be tilted so that the propellers are clear of thrown-up water. They are 600 h.p. Junkers Jumo Diesel engines and give a top speed of 208 m.p.h. and a maximum range of 5600 miles at 130 m.p.h.

SOME ITALIAN AIRCRAFT

Fiat C.R. 42

This fighter biplane differs noticeably from the British Gloster Gladiator in having wings of unequal span, an open cockpit, and interplane strutting of the W girder type. The supercharged 840 h.p. radial engine is said to give a top speed of 270 m.p.h.

The armament consists of two heavy machine guns. There are spats over the wheels. Fiat C.R. 42 fighters accompanied the Italian bombers which twice crossed the British coast in the summer of 1940.

The Macchi C. 200 is a low-wing single-seater monoplane fighter. It has the Fiat 840 radial engine which gives it a top speed of 313 m.p.h. The undercarriage retracts inwards. The armament consists of two 12.7 mm. heavy machine guns firing through the airscrew. The Macchi C. 200 is the fastest Italian single-seater fighter.

The Breda 88 is a twin-engined high-wing monoplane which can be used, like the Me. 110, as a fighter or light bomber. Two Piaggio 1000 h.p. radial engines give a top speed of 320 m.p.h. The wings taper from the trailing edge, and there are twin fins and rudders. The undercarriage retracts into the engine nacelles. The armament consists of fixed guns in the nose and movable guns mounted at the rear of the cabin.

The Savoia-Marchetti S.M. 79 is a low-wing bomber with three radial Bristol engines built by the Alfa-Romeo company, giving a top speed of 270 m.p.h. There is a humped cabin. The undercarriage retracts into the outer engine nacelles. The armament consists of three heavy machine guns.

The Fiat B.R. 20 is a low-wing monoplane heavy bomber. Two Fiat 1000 h.p. radial engines give a top speed of 270 m.p.h. There are twin fins and rudders.

The armament consists of a heavy machine gun in a power-operated turret in the nose, another in a power-operated turret above the fuselage, and a third heavy machine gun to fire below. Fiat B.R. 20 bombers made two attempts to intervene in the battle of Britain in November 1940 which proved disastrous for them.

The Cant Z 501 flying boat is of rather obsolete design. There is a high wing of 74-foot span carried above the boat by a complicated array of struts. In the center of the wing is mounted a liquid-cooled Isotta-Fraschini 900 h.p. engine, giving the boat a top speed of 170 m.p.h.

In the engine nacelle is a rear gunner position. There is a gun in the bows and another amidships.

The Cant Z 506B is a three-engined seaplane of great size. The wings have a span of 86 feet 11 inches. There are twin floats. The three radial engines are said to give a top speed of over 230 m.p.h.